THE BLESSINGS OF LIBERTY

THE BLESSINGS OF LIBERTY

Readings for the 2022 HUMANITAS SUMMER SYMPOSIUM

Selected and edited by
THE PORTSMOUTH INSTITUTE FOR FAITH AND CULTURE

CLUNY
Providence, Rhode Island

For more information about Cluny,
please visit WWW.CLUNYMEDIA.COM.

For more information on the Humanities Program at Providence College,
please visit WWW.HUMANITIES.PROVIDENCE.EDU.

For more information on The Portsmouth Institute for Faith and Culture,
please visit WWW.PORTSMOUTHINSTITUTE.ORG.

Cover design by Clarke & Clarke
Cover image: Hans Hartig, *The Next Morning,*
1912, oil on canvas
Courtesy of Wikimedia Commons

ACKNOWLEDGMENTS

Excerpts of St. Paul, *Letter to the Romans*, are from the Revised Standard Version of the Bible—Second Catholic Edition (Ignatius Edition), copyright © 2006 National Council of the Churches of Christ in the United States of America. All rights reserved.

Excerpts of St. Augustine, *The Confessions* are from the 1998 Vintage edition, translated by Maria Boulding, O.S.B. All rights reserved.

Excerpts of Thomas More, *Letter to William Gonell* are from the 1928 Burns & Oates edition of Thomas Stapleton's *The Life and Illustrious Martyrdom of Sir Thomas More*.

Excerpts of St. Benedict, *The Rule of St. Benedict* are from the 1953 Newman Press edition.

Excerpts of James Madison, *Federalist 51* are from the 1961 Wesleyan University Press edition of *The Federalist Papers*.

Excerpts of St. Thomas Aquinas, *Summa Theologiae* are from the 1920 edition of the Fathers of the English Dominican Province, courtesy of New Advent and Kevin Knight. All rights reserved.

Nathaniel Hawthorne, "My Kinsman, Major Molineux," is from the 2018 Cluny edition of *The Shattered Fountain: Selected Tales of Nathaniel Hawthorne*. All rights reserved.

Excerpts of Alexis de Tocqueville, *The Old Regime and the French Revolution* are from the 1856 Harper and Brothers edition.

Excerpts of C. S. Lewis, *The Screwtape Letters* are from the 1944 Geoffrey Bles / Centenary Press edition. All rights reserved.

Excerpts of Pope John Paul II, *Veritatis Splendor* are from the 2022 Libreria Editrice Vaticana (online) edition. All rights reserved.

Excerpts of Josef Pieper, *Leisure, the Basis of Culture* are from the 2009 Ignatius Press edition. All rights reserved.

COURSE OF READINGS

Introduction

CHRISTOPHER FISHER

*W*hat is liberty?

I pose this question to my students at the conclusion of each work we read in our signature Humanities Program at Portsmouth Abbey School.

What is liberty according to Augustine's Confessions? *Or, what is liberty according to John Locke's* Second Treatise? *Even, what is liberty according to Marx's* Communist Manifesto *and* Freud's *Civilization and Its Discontents?*

I ask my students to repeatedly consider this question because liberty is at the very heart of human existence—and thus the Christian and Western intellectual tradition, which attempts to understand and articulate its meaning. The centrality of liberty to human flourishing is a truth—perhaps the only truth—which Justice Anthony Kennedy grasped in his opinion in *Planned Parenthood v. Casey*, when he succinctly summarized the modern conception of liberty as "the right to define one's own concept of existence, of meaning, of the universe, and of the mystery of human life."

Kennedy rightly perceives what is at stake in a civilization's definition of liberty. Unfortunately, while expressing the milieu in which it was written, Kennedy's remark fails to draw on the sources which, for over more than two millennia, have formed our understanding of liberty as a central human value. It is this deeper and broader tradition rejected by Kennedy which allows us to contemplate liberty in relation to something outside of ourselves, to fully understand this superhuman power which we humans have nonetheless been granted. In failing to understand liberty, Kennedy fails to understand human nature and human ends.

Amid the fog which the modern confusion surrounding liberty has wafted upon us, I invite my students to engage in the quest for true liberty, to know its true meaning, to grasp its true causes, to contemplate its true ends. I invite my students to seek the true light of liberty, one illumed by Christ, from whom we receive liberty—as the American Founders suggested—as a blessing. For, as Christ himself told his disciples, "If you continue in my word, you are truly my disciples; and you will know the truth, and the truth will make you free" (John 8:31–32).

At the Portsmouth Institute's 2022 Summer Symposium on *The Blessings of Liberty*, you too are invited to once again be a student as together we search for the true meaning of liberty and examine how liberty has been understood in the

West from St. Paul to the American Founders, to giants of the twentieth-century Catholic intellectual renewal. Many of the works excerpted in this volume feature prominently in Portsmouth Abbey's innovative Humanities curriculum.

Our aim is to come away from the weekend with a surer foundation on which we can understand liberty, and consider it across various contexts: in political and economic life, in our families, in the Church, and as a goal of Catholic education. In addition to discovering the ancient and modern sources for thinking about the meaning of liberty, we will take time to examine our own present day, and how we can best live up to our nation's promise to "secure the Blessings of Liberty to ourselves and our Posterity."

We look forward to enjoying a weekend of stimulating conversation, convivial friendship, and prayerful leisure with you.

Christopher Fisher
PORTSMOUTH ABBEY
EASTER 2022

PART I
Liberty and the Soul

Letter to the Romans

ST. PAUL

CHAPTER 4

(1) What then shall we say about Abraham, our forefather according to the flesh? (2) For if Abraham was justified by works, he has something to boast about, but not before God. (3) For what does the scripture say? "Abraham believed God, and it was reckoned to him as righteousness." (4) Now to one who works, his wages are not reckoned as a gift but as his due. (5) And to one who does not work but trusts him who justifies the ungodly, his faith is reckoned as righteousness. (6) So also David pronounces a blessing upon the man to whom God reckons righteousness apart from works:

> (7) "Blessed are those whose iniquities are forgiven, and whose sins are covered;
> (8) blessed is the man against whom the Lord will not reckon his sin."

(9) Is this blessing pronounced only upon the circumcised, or also upon the uncircumcised? We say that faith was reckoned to Abraham as righteousness. (10) How then was it reckoned to him? Was it before or after he had been circumcised? It was not after, but before he was circumcised. (11) He received circumcision as a sign or seal of the righteousness which he had by faith while he was still uncircumcised. The purpose was to make him the father of all who believe without being circumcised and who thus have righteousness reckoned to them, (12) and likewise the father of the circumcised who are not merely circumcised but also follow the example of the faith which our father Abraham had before he was circumcised.

(13) The promise to Abraham and his descendants, that they should inherit the world, did not come through the law but through the righteousness of faith. (14) If it is the adherents of the law who are to be the heirs, faith is null and the promise is void. (15) For the law brings wrath, but where there is no law there is no transgression.

(16) That is why it depends on faith, in order that the promise may rest on grace and be guaranteed to all his descendants—not only to the adherents of the law but also to those who share the faith of Abraham, for he is the father of us all, (17) as it is written, "I have made you the father of many nations"—in the presence of the God in whom he believed, who gives life to the dead and calls into existence the things that do not exist. (18) In hope he believed against hope, that he should become the father of many nations; as he had been

told, "So shall your descendants be." (19) He did not weaken in faith when he considered his own body, which was as good as dead because he was about a hundred years old, or when he considered the barrenness of Sarah's womb. (20) No distrust made him waver concerning the promise of God, but he grew strong in his faith as he gave glory to God, (21) fully convinced that God was able to do what he had promised. (22) That is why his faith was "reckoned to him as righteousness." (23) But the words, "it was reckoned to him," were written not for his sake alone, (24) but for ours also. It will be reckoned to us who believe in him that raised from the dead Jesus our Lord, (25) who was put to death for our trespasses and raised for our justification.

CHAPTER 5

(1) Therefore, since we are justified by faith, we have peace with God through our Lord Jesus Christ. (2) Through him we have obtained access to this grace in which we stand, and we rejoice in our hope of sharing the glory of God. (3) More than that, we rejoice in our sufferings, knowing that suffering produces endurance, (4) and endurance produces character, and character produces hope, (5) and hope does not disappoint us, because God's love has been poured into our hearts through the Holy Spirit which has been given to us.

(6) While we were still weak, at the right time Christ died for the ungodly. (7) Why, one will hardly die for a righteous

man—though perhaps for a good man one will dare even to die. (8) But God shows his love for us in that while we were yet sinners Christ died for us. (9) Since, therefore, we are now justified by his blood, much more shall we be saved by him from the wrath of God. (10) For if while we were enemies we were reconciled to God by the death of his Son, much more, now that we are reconciled, shall we be saved by his life. (11) Not only so, but we also rejoice in God through our Lord Jesus Christ, through whom we have now received our reconciliation.

(12) Therefore as sin came into the world through one man and death through sin, and so death spread to all men because all men sinned—(13) sin indeed was in the world before the law was given, but sin is not counted where there is no law. (14) Yet death reigned from Adam to Moses, even over those whose sins were not like the transgression of Adam, who was a type of the one who was to come.

(15) But the free gift is not like the trespass. For if many died through one man's trespass, much more have the grace of God and the free gift in the grace of that one man Jesus Christ abounded for many. (16) And the free gift is not like the effect of that one man's sin. For the judgment following one trespass brought condemnation, but the free gift following many trespasses brings justification. (17) If, because of one man's trespass, death reigned through that one man, much more will those who receive the abundance of grace and the free gift of righteousness reign in life through the one man Jesus Christ.

(18) Then as one man's trespass led to condemnation for all men, so one man's act of righteousness leads to acquittal and life for all men. (19) For as by one man's disobedience many were made sinners, so by one man's obedience many will be made righteous. (20) Law came in, to increase the trespass; but where sin increased, grace abounded all the more, (21) so that, as sin reigned in death, grace also might reign through righteousness to eternal life through Jesus Christ our Lord.

CHAPTER 6

(1) What shall we say then? Are we to continue in sin that grace may abound? (2) By no means! How can we who died to sin still live in it? (3) Do you not know that all of us who have been baptized into Christ Jesus were baptized into his death? (4) We were buried therefore with him by baptism into death, so that as Christ was raised from the dead by the glory of the Father, we too might walk in newness of life.

(5) For if we have been united with him in a death like his, we shall certainly be united with him in a resurrection like his. (6) We know that our old self was crucified with him so that the sinful body might be destroyed, and we might no longer be enslaved to sin. (7) For he who has died is freed from sin. (8) But if we have died with Christ, we believe that we shall also live with him. (9) For we know that Christ being raised from the dead will never die again; death no longer has

dominion over him. (10) The death he died he died to sin, once for all, but the life he lives he lives to God. (11) So you also must consider yourselves dead to sin and alive to God in Christ Jesus.

(12) Let not sin therefore reign in your mortal bodies, to make you obey their passions. (13) Do not yield your members to sin as instruments of wickedness, but yield yourselves to God as men who have been brought from death to life, and your members to God as instruments of righteousness. (14) For sin will have no dominion over you, since you are not under law but under grace.

(15) What then? Are we to sin because we are not under law but under grace? By no means! (16) Do you not know that if you yield yourselves to any one as obedient slaves, you are slaves of the one whom you obey, either of sin, which leads to death, or of obedience, which leads to righteousness? (17) But thanks be to God, that you who were once slaves of sin have become obedient from the heart to the standard of teaching to which you were committed, (18) and, having been set free from sin, have become slaves of righteousness. (19) I am speaking in human terms, because of your natural limitations. For just as you once yielded your members to impurity and to greater and greater iniquity, so now yield your members to righteousness for sanctification.

(20) When you were slaves of sin, you were free in regard to righteousness. (21) But then what return did you get from the things of which you are now ashamed? The end of those

things is death. (22) But now that you have been set free from sin and have become slaves of God, the return you get is sanctification and its end, eternal life. (23) For the wages of sin is death, but the free gift of God is eternal life in Christ Jesus our Lord.

CHAPTER 7

(1) Do you not know, brethren—for I am speaking to those who know the law—that the law is binding on a person only during his life? (2) Thus a married woman is bound by law to her husband as long as he lives; but if her husband dies she is discharged from the law concerning the husband. (3) Accordingly, she will be called an adulteress if she lives with another man while her husband is alive. But if her husband dies she is free from that law, and if she marries another man she is not an adulteress.

(4) Likewise, my brethren, you have died to the law through the body of Christ, so that you may belong to another, to him who has been raised from the dead in order that we may bear fruit for God. (5) While we were living in the flesh, our sinful passions, aroused by the law, were at work in our members to bear fruit for death. (6) But now we are discharged from the law, dead to that which held us captive, so that we serve not under the old written code but in the new life of the Spirit.

(7) What then shall we say? That the law is sin? By no

means! Yet, if it had not been for the law, I should not have
known sin. I should not have known what it is to covet if the
law had not said, "You shall not covet." (8) But sin, finding
opportunity in the commandment, wrought in me all kinds
of covetousness. Apart from the law sin lies dead. (9) I was
once alive apart from the law, but when the commandment
came, sin revived and I died; (10) the very commandment
which promised life proved to be death to me. (11) For sin,
finding opportunity in the commandment, deceived me and
by it killed me. (12) So the law is holy, and the commandment is holy and just and good.

(13) Did that which is good, then, bring death to me? By
no means! It was sin, working death in me through what is
good, in order that sin might be shown to be sin, and through
the commandment might become sinful beyond measure.
(14) We know that the law is spiritual; but I am carnal, sold
under sin. (15) I do not understand my own actions. For I do
not do what I want, but I do the very thing I hate. (16) Now
if I do what I do not want, I agree that the law is good. (17)
So then it is no longer I that do it, but sin which dwells within
me. (18) For I know that nothing good dwells within me, that
is, in my flesh. I can will what is right, but I cannot do it. (19)
For I do not do the good I want, but the evil I do not want is
what I do. (20) Now if I do what I do not want, it is no longer
I that do it, but sin which dwells within me.

(21) So I find it to be a law that when I want to do right,
evil lies close at hand. (22) For I delight in the law of God, in

my inmost self, (23) but I see in my members another law at war with the law of my mind and making me captive to the law of sin which dwells in my members. (24) Wretched man that I am! Who will deliver me from this body of death? (25) Thanks be to God through Jesus Christ our Lord! So then, I of myself serve the law of God with my mind, but with my flesh I serve the law of sin.

CHAPTER 8

(1) There is therefore now no condemnation for those who are in Christ Jesus. (2) For the law of the Spirit of life in Christ Jesus has set me free from the law of sin and death. (3) For God has done what the law, weakened by the flesh, could not do: sending his own Son in the likeness of sinful flesh and for sin, he condemned sin in the flesh, (4) in order that the just requirement of the law might be fulfilled in us, who walk not according to the flesh but according to the Spirit. (5) For those who live according to the flesh set their minds on the things of the flesh, but those who live according to the Spirit set their minds on the things of the Spirit. (6) To set the mind on the flesh is death, but to set the mind on the Spirit is life and peace. (7) For the mind that is set on the flesh is hostile to God; it does not submit to God's law, indeed it cannot; (8) and those who are in the flesh cannot please God.

(9) But you are not in the flesh, you are in the Spirit, if in fact the Spirit of God dwells in you. Any one who does not

have the Spirit of Christ does not belong to him. (10) But if Christ is in you, although your bodies are dead because of sin, your spirits are alive because of righteousness. (11) If the Spirit of him who raised Jesus from the dead dwells in you, he who raised Christ Jesus from the dead will give life to your mortal bodies also through his Spirit which dwells in you.

(12) So then, brethren, we are debtors, not to the flesh, to live according to the flesh—(13) for if you live according to the flesh you will die, but if by the Spirit you put to death the deeds of the body you will live. (14) For all who are led by the Spirit of God are sons of God. (15) For you did not receive the spirit of slavery to fall back into fear, but you have received the spirit of sonship. When we cry, "Abba! Father!" (16) it is the Spirit himself bearing witness with our spirit that we are children of God, (17) and if children, then heirs, heirs of God and fellow heirs with Christ, provided we suffer with him in order that we may also be glorified with him.

(18) I consider that the sufferings of this present time are not worth comparing with the glory that is to be revealed to us. (19) For the creation waits with eager longing for the revealing of the sons of God; (20) for the creation was subjected to futility, not of its own will but by the will of him who subjected it in hope; (21) because the creation itself will be set free from its bondage to decay and obtain the glorious liberty of the children of God. (22) We know that the whole creation has been groaning in travail together until now; (23) and not only the creation, but we ourselves, who have the first

fruits of the Spirit, groan inwardly as we wait for adoption as sons, the redemption of our bodies. (24) For in this hope we were saved. Now hope that is seen is not hope. For who hopes for what he sees? (25) But if we hope for what we do not see, we wait for it with patience.

(26) Likewise the Spirit helps us in our weakness; for we do not know how to pray as we ought, but the Spirit himself intercedes for us with sighs too deep for words. (27) And he who searches the hearts of men knows what is the mind of the Spirit, because the Spirit intercedes for the saints according to the will of God.

(28) We know that in everything God works for good with those who love him, who are called according to his purpose. (29) For those whom he foreknew he also predestined to be conformed to the image of his Son, in order that he might be the first-born among many brethren. (30) And those whom he predestined he also called; and those whom he called he also justified; and those whom he justified he also glorified.

(31) What then shall we say to this? If God is for us, who is against us? (32) He who did not spare his own Son but gave him up for us all, will he not also give us all things with him? (32) Who shall bring any charge against God's elect? It is God who justifies; (34) who is to condemn? Is it Christ Jesus, who died, yes, who was raised from the dead, who is at the right hand of God, who indeed intercedes for us? (35) Who shall separate us from the love of Christ? Shall tribulation, or

distress, or persecution, or famine, or nakedness, or peril, or sword? (36) As it is written,

"For thy sake we are being killed all the day long;
we are regarded as sheep to be slaughtered."

(37) No, in all these things we are more than conquerors through him who loved us. (38) For I am sure that neither death, nor life, nor angels, nor principalities, nor things present, nor things to come, nor powers, (39) nor height, nor depth, nor anything else in all creation, will be able to separate us from the love of God in Christ Jesus our Lord.

CHAPTER 9

(1) I am speaking the truth in Christ, I am not lying; my conscience bears me witness in the Holy Spirit, (2) that I have great sorrow and unceasing anguish in my heart. (3) For I could wish that I myself were accursed and cut off from Christ for the sake of my brethren, my kinsmen by race. (4) They are Israelites, and to them belong the sonship, the glory, the covenants, the giving of the law, the worship, and the promises; (5) to them belong the patriarchs, and of their race, according to the flesh, is the Christ. God who is over all be blessed for ever. Amen.

(6) But it is not as though the word of God had failed. For not all who are descended from Israel belong to Israel,

(7) and not all are children of Abraham because they are his descendants; but "Through Isaac shall your descendants be named." (8) This means that it is not the children of the flesh who are the children of God, but the children of the promise are reckoned as descendants. (9) For this is what the promise said, "About this time I will return and Sarah shall have a son." (10) And not only so, but also when Rebecca had conceived children by one man, our forefather Isaac, (11) though they were not yet born and had done nothing either good or bad, in order that God's purpose of election might continue, not because of works but because of his call, (12) she was told, "The elder will serve the younger." (13) As it is written, "Jacob I loved, but Esau I hated."

(14) What shall we say then? Is there injustice on God's part? By no means! (15) For he says to Moses, "I will have mercy on whom I have mercy, and I will have compassion on whom I have compassion." (16) So it depends not upon man's will or exertion, but upon God's mercy. (17) For the scripture says to Pharaoh, "I have raised you up for the very purpose of showing my power in you, so that my name may be proclaimed in all the earth." (18) So then he has mercy upon whomever he wills, and he hardens the heart of whomever he wills.

(19) You will say to me then, "Why does he still find fault? For who can resist his will?" (20) But who are you, a man, to answer back to God? Will what is molded say to its molder, "Why have you made me thus?" (21) Has the potter

no right over the clay, to make out of the same lump one ves-
sel for beauty and another for menial use? (22) What if God,
desiring to show his wrath and to make known his power, has
endured with much patience the vessels of wrath made for
destruction, (23) in order to make known the riches of his
glory for the vessels of mercy, which he has prepared beforehand for glory, (24) even us whom he has called, not from the
Jews only but also from the Gentiles? (25) As indeed he says
in Hosea,

> "Those who were not my people
> I will call 'my people,'
> and her who was not beloved
> I will call 'my beloved.'"
> (26) "And in the very place where it was said to them,
> 'You are not my people,'
> they will be called 'sons of the living God.' "

(27) And Isaiah cries out concerning Israel: "Though the
number of the sons of Israel be as the sand of the sea, only a
remnant of them will be saved; (28) for the Lord will execute
his sentence upon the earth with rigor and dispatch." (29)
And as Isaiah predicted,

> "If the Lord of hosts had not left us children,
> we would have fared like Sodom and been made like
> Gomorrah."

(30) What shall we say, then? That Gentiles who did not pursue righteousness have attained it, that is, righteousness through faith; (31) but that Israel who pursued the righteousness which is based on law did not succeed in fulfilling that law. (32) Why? Because they did not pursue it through faith, but as if it were based on works. They have stumbled over the stumbling stone, (32) as it is written,

> "Behold, I am laying in Zion a stone that will make men
> stumble,
> a rock that will make them fall;
> and he who believes in him will not be put to shame."

CHAPTER 10

(1) Brethren, my heart's desire and prayer to God for them is that they may be saved. (2) I bear them witness that they have a zeal for God, but it is not enlightened. (3) For, being ignorant of the righteousness that comes from God, and seeking to establish their own, they did not submit to God's righteousness. (4) For Christ is the end of the law, that every one who has faith may be justified.

(5) Moses writes that the man who practices the righteousness which is based on the law shall live by it. (6) But the righteousness based on faith says, Do not say in your heart, "Who will ascend into heaven?" (that is, to bring Christ down) (7) or "Who will descend into the abyss?" (that is,

to bring Christ up from the dead). (8) But what does it say?
The word is near you, on your lips and in your heart (that
is, the word of faith which we preach); (9) because, if you
confess with your lips that Jesus is Lord and believe in your
heart that God raised him from the dead, you will be saved.
(10) For man believes with his heart and so is justified, and
he confesses with his lips and so is saved. (11) The scripture
says, "No one who believes in him will be put to shame." (12)
For there is no distinction between Jew and Greek; the same
Lord is Lord of all and bestows his riches upon all who call
upon him. (13) For, "every one who calls upon the name of
the Lord will be saved."

(14) But how are men to call upon him in whom they
have not believed? And how are they to believe in him of
whom they have never heard? And how are they to hear without a preacher? (15) And how can men preach unless they
are sent? As it is written, "How beautiful are the feet of those
who preach good news!" (16) But they have not all obeyed the
gospel; for Isaiah says, "Lord, who has believed what he has
heard from us?" (17) So faith comes from what is heard, and
what is heard comes by the preaching of Christ.

(18) But I ask, have they not heard? Indeed they have; for

"Their voice has gone out to all the earth,
and their words to the ends of the world."

(19) Again I ask, did Israel not understand? First Moses says,

"I will make you jealous of those who are not a nation;
with a foolish nation I will make you angry."

(20) Then Isaiah is so bold as to say,

"I have been found by those who did not seek me;
I have shown myself to those who did not ask for me."

(21) But of Israel he says, "All day long I have held out my hands to a disobedient and contrary people."

CHAPTER 11

(1) I ask, then, has God rejected his people? By no means! I myself am an Israelite, a descendant of Abraham, a member of the tribe of Benjamin. (2) God has not rejected his people whom he foreknew. Do you not know what the scripture says of Elijah, how he pleads with God against Israel? (3) "Lord, they have killed thy prophets, they have demolished thy altars, and I alone am left, and they seek my life." (4) But what is God's reply to him? "I have kept for myself seven thousand men who have not bowed the knee to Baal." (5) So too at the present time there is a remnant, chosen by grace. (6) But if it is by grace, it is no longer on the basis of works; otherwise grace would no longer be grace.

(7) What then? Israel failed to obtain what it sought. The elect obtained it, but the rest were hardened, (8) as it is written,

"God gave them a spirit of stupor,
eyes that should not see and ears that should not hear,
down to this very day."

(9) And David says,

"Let their table become a snare and a trap,
a pitfall and a retribution for them;
(10) let their eyes be darkened so that they cannot see,
and bend their backs for ever."

(11) So I ask, have they stumbled so as to fall? By no means! But through their trespass salvation has come to the Gentiles, so as to make Israel jealous. (12) Now if their trespass means riches for the world, and if their failure means riches for the Gentiles, how much more will their full inclusion mean!

(13) Now I am speaking to you Gentiles. Inasmuch then as I am an apostle to the Gentiles, I magnify my ministry (14) in order to make my fellow Jews jealous, and thus save some of them. (15) For if their rejection means the reconciliation of the world, what will their acceptance mean but life from the dead? (16) If the dough offered as first fruits is holy, so is the whole lump; and if the root is holy, so are the branches.

(17) But if some of the branches were broken off, and you, a wild olive shoot, were grafted in their place to share the richness of the olive tree, (18) do not boast over the branches. If you do boast, remember it is not you that support the root,

but the root that supports you. (19) You will say, "Branches were broken off so that I might be grafted in." (20) That is true. They were broken off because of their unbelief, but you stand fast only through faith. So do not become proud, but stand in awe. (21) For if God did not spare the natural branches, neither will he spare you. (22) Note then the kindness and the severity of God: severity toward those who have fallen, but God's kindness to you, provided you continue in his kindness; otherwise you too will be cut off. (23) And even the others, if they do not persist in their unbelief, will be grafted in, for God has the power to graft them in again. (24) For if you have been cut from what is by nature a wild olive tree, and grafted, contrary to nature, into a cultivated olive tree, how much more will these natural branches be grafted back into their own olive tree.

(25) Lest you be wise in your own conceits, I want you to understand this mystery, brethren: a hardening has come upon part of Israel, until the full number of the Gentiles come in, (26) and so all Israel will be saved; as it is written,

> "The Deliverer will come from Zion,
> he will banish ungodliness from Jacob";
> (27) "and this will be my covenant with them
> when I take away their sins."

(28) As regards the gospel they are enemies of God, for your sake; but as regards election they are beloved for the sake

of their forefathers. (29) For the gifts and the call of God are irrevocable. (30) Just as you were once disobedient to God but now have received mercy because of their disobedience, (31) so they have now been disobedient in order that by the mercy shown to you they also may receive mercy. (32) For God has consigned all men to disobedience, that he may have mercy upon all.

(32) O the depth of the riches and wisdom and knowledge of God! How unsearchable are his judgments and how inscrutable his ways!

(34) "For who has known the mind of the Lord,
or who has been his counselor?"
(35) "Or who has given a gift to him
that he might be repaid?"

(36) For from him and through him and to him are all things. To him be glory for ever. Amen.

CHAPTER 12

(1) I appeal to you therefore, brethren, by the mercies of God, to present your bodies as a living sacrifice, holy and acceptable to God, which is your spiritual worship. (2) Do not be conformed to this world but be transformed by the renewal of your mind, that you may prove what is the will of God, what is good and acceptable and perfect.

(3) For by the grace given to me I bid every one among you not to think of himself more highly than he ought to think, but to think with sober judgment, each according to the measure of faith which God has assigned him. (4) For as in one body we have many members, and all the members do not have the same function, (5) so we, though many, are one body in Christ, and individually members one of another. (6) Having gifts that differ according to the grace given to us, let us use them: if prophecy, in proportion to our faith; (7) if service, in our serving; he who teaches, in his teaching; (8) he who exhorts, in his exhortation; he who contributes, in liberality; he who gives aid, with zeal; he who does acts of mercy, with cheerfulness.

(9) Let love be genuine; hate what is evil, hold fast to what is good; (10) love one another with brotherly affection; outdo one another in showing honor. (11) Never flag in zeal, be aglow with the Spirit, serve the Lord. (12) Rejoice in your hope, be patient in tribulation, be constant in prayer. (13) Contribute to the needs of the saints, practice hospitality.

(14) Bless those who persecute you; bless and do not curse them. (15) Rejoice with those who rejoice, weep with those who weep. (16) Live in harmony with one another; do not be haughty, but associate with the lowly; never be conceited. (17) Repay no one evil for evil, but take thought for what is noble in the sight of all. (18) If possible, so far as it depends upon you, live peaceably with all. (19) Beloved, never avenge yourselves, but leave it to the wrath of God; for it is written,

"Vengeance is mine, I will repay, says the Lord." (20) No, "if your enemy is hungry, feed him; if he is thirsty, give him drink; for by so doing you will heap burning coals upon his head." (21) Do not be overcome by evil, but overcome evil with good.

CHAPTER 13

(1) Let every person be subject to the governing authorities. For there is no authority except from God, and those that exist have been instituted by God. (2) Therefore he who resists the authorities resists what God has appointed, and those who resist will incur judgment. (3) For rulers are not a terror to good conduct, but to bad. Would you have no fear of him who is in authority? Then do what is good, and you will receive his approval, (4) for he is God's servant for your good. But if you do wrong, be afraid, for he does not bear the sword in vain; he is the servant of God to execute his wrath on the wrongdoer. (5) Therefore one must be subject, not only to avoid God's wrath but also for the sake of conscience. (6) For the same reason you also pay taxes, for the authorities are ministers of God, attending to this very thing. (7) Pay all of them their dues, taxes to whom taxes are due, revenue to whom revenue is due, respect to whom respect is due, honor to whom honor is due.

(8) Owe no one anything, except to love one another; for he who loves his neighbor has fulfilled the law. (9) The

commandments, "You shall not commit adultery, You shall not kill, You shall not steal, You shall not covet," and any other commandment, are summed up in this sentence, "You shall love your neighbor as yourself." (10) Love does no wrong to a neighbor; therefore love is the fulfilling of the law.

(11) Besides this you know what hour it is, how it is full time now for you to wake from sleep. For salvation is nearer to us now than when we first believed; (12) the night is far gone, the day is at hand. Let us then cast off the works of darkness and put on the armor of light; (13) let us conduct ourselves becomingly as in the day, not in reveling and drunkenness, not in debauchery and licentiousness, not in quarreling and jealousy. (14) But put on the Lord Jesus Christ, and make no provision for the flesh, to gratify its desires.

notes

_____

_____

_____

_____

_____

_____

_____

_____

_____

_____

_____

_____

_____

_____

_____

_____

_____

_____

_____

_____

notes

The Confessions

ST. AUGUSTINE

BOOK VIII: CONVERSION

1, 1. In a spirit of thankfulness let me recall the mercies you lavished on me, O my God; to you let me confess them.[1] May I be flooded with love for you until my very bones cry out, "Who is like you, O Lord?"[2] Let me offer you a sacrifice of praise, for you have snapped my bonds.[3] How you broke them I will relate, so that all your worshipers who hear my tale may exclaim, "Blessed be the Lord, blessed in heaven and on earth, for great and wonderful is his name."[4]

Your words were now firmly implanted in my heart of hearts, and I was besieged by you on every side.[5] Concerning

---

1. See Ps 85 (86):13; Is 63:7.
2. See Ps 34 (35):10.
3. See Ps 115 (116):16–17.
4. See Ps 134 (135):6; 75:2 (76:1); 8:2 (1).
5. See Is 29:2.

33

your eternal life I was now quite certain, though I had but glimpsed it like a tantalizing reflection in a mirror[6]; this had been enough to take from me any lingering doubt concerning that imperishable substance from which every other substance derives its being. What I now longed for was not greater certainty about you, but a more steadfast abiding in you. In my daily life everything seemed to be teetering, and my heart needed to be cleansed of the old leaven.[7] I was attracted to the Way, which is our Savior himself, but the narrowness of the path daunted me and I still could not walk in it.[8]

You inspired in me the idea that I ought to go to Simplicianus, and even I could see the sense of this. I regarded him as your good servant, a man from whom grace radiated. Moreover I had heard how from his youth he had lived for you in complete dedication, and since he was an old man by now I assumed that after following your way of life for long years and with such noble zeal he must be rich in experience and deeply learned. And so indeed he was. I hoped, therefore, that if I could discuss my perplexities with him he would bring out from his storehouse[9] appropriate advice as to how a man in my condition might walk in your way.

2. Surveying the full assembly of the Church I observed that people's lifestyles varied. For my own part I was irked

6. See 1 Cor 13:12.
7. See 1 Cor 5:7–8.
8. See Mt 7:14.
9. See Mt 13:52.

by the secular business I was conducting, for no longer was I fired by ambition, and prepared on that account to endure such heavy servitude in the hope of reputation and wealth, as had formerly been the case. Those prospects held no charm for me now that I was in love with your tender kindness and the beauty of your house[10]; but I was in tight bondage to a woman. The apostle did not forbid me to marry, although he did propose a better choice, earnestly wishing that everyone might live as he did himself[11]; but I was too weak for that and inclined to an easier course. For this reason alone I was vacillating, bored and listless amid my shriveled cares because I was forced to adapt myself to other aspects of conjugal life to which I had pledged and constrained myself, though they were little to my liking. From the lips of your Truth I had heard that *there are eunuchs who have castrated themselves for love of the kingdom of heaven*, but the saying continues, *Let anyone accept this who can.*[12]

How foolish are they who know not God! So many good things before their eyes, yet *Him Who Is* they fail to see.[13] I was trapped in that foolishness no longer, for I had left it behind by hearkening to the concerted witness of your whole creation, and had discovered you, our creator, and your Word, who dwells with you and is with you the one sole God,

---

10. See Ps 25 (26):18.
11. See 1 Cor 7:7–8.
12. Mt 19:12.
13. See Wis 13:1.

through whom you have created all things.[14] But there are impious people of another type, who do recognize God yet have not glorified him as God, nor given him thanks.[15] Into that error too I had formerly blundered, but your right hand grasped me,[16] plucked me out of it and put me in a place where I could be healed, for you have told us that *reverence for God—that is wisdom,*[17] and warned *us, Do not give yourself airs for wisdom,* because *those who believed themselves wise have sunk into folly.*[18] I had found a precious pearl, worth buying at the cost of all I had[19]; but I went on hesitating.

Conversation with Simplicianus

2, 3. Accordingly I made my way to Simplicianus. When Ambrose, then bishop, had been baptized, Simplicianus had stood as father to him, and Ambrose regarded him with affection as a father indeed. To him I described the winding paths of my wayward life. When I mentioned that I had read certain Platonist books, translated into Latin by Victorinus, who had formerly been a rhetorician in Rome but had, as I had heard, died a Christian, Simplicianus told me how fortunate I was not to have stumbled on the writings of other philosophers,

---

14. See Jn 1:1–3.
15. See Rom 1:21.
16. See Ps 117:36 (118:35).
17. Jb 28:28.
18. Prv 26:5; Rom 1:22.
19. See Mt 13:46; 19:21.

works full of fallacies and dishonesty that smacked of the principles of this world,[20] whereas those Platonist writings conveyed in every possible way, albeit indirectly, the truth of God and his Word.

Story of Victorinus' conversion

He went on to reminisce about this Victorious with the object of inculcating in me that humility of Christ which is hidden from the sagacious but revealed to little ones.[21] He knew him intimately in Rome, and he told me a story about Victorious which I will not pass over in silence, since it powerfully redounds to the praise of your grace and moves me to confession, this story of a deeply learned old man.

Thoroughly conversant with all the liberal arts, Victorinus had also read widely and with discrimination in philosophy and had taught many a noble senator; in recognition of his distinction as a teacher a statue had been erected to him in the Roman forum, which was a very high honor in the eyes of worldly people, and one he well deserved. Until this period of his life he had been a worshiper of idols and shared the abominable superstitions which at that time blew like an ill wind through almost the whole of the Roman nobility, who were agog for Pelusium and for

---

20.   See Col 2:8.
21.   See Mt 11:25.

Anubis, dog-voiced god, and monstrous deities
of many a hue, who warred in days gone by
against Minerva, Neptune, Venus....

These gods Rome had once vanquished, but now worshiped, and the elderly Victorinus with his terrible thunders had habitually defended their cults; yet he was not ashamed to become a child of Christ and be born as an infant from your font, bending his neck to the yoke of humility[22] and accepting on his docile brow the sign o: the ignominious cross.[23]

4. O Lord, Lord, who bade your heavens stoop, who touched the mountains and set them smoking,[24] by what means did you make your hidden way into that man's breast? The story as Simplicianus told it to me was this. Victorinus was in the habit of reading holy scripture and intensively studying all the Christian writings, which he subjected to close scrutiny; and he would say to Simplicianus, not openly but in private, intimate conversation, "I am already a Christian, you know." But the other always replied, "I will not believe that, nor count you among Christians, until I see you in Christ's Church." Victorinus would chaff him: "It's the walls that make Christians, then?" He would often talk like this, claiming that he was a Christian. Simplicianus often

22. See Sir 51:34; Jer 27:12; Mt 11:29.
23. See Gal 5:11.
24. See Ps 143 (144):5.

responded in the same way, and Victorinus would frequently repeat his joke about walls.

The fact was that he was sorely afraid of upsetting the proud demon-worshipers who were his friends, fearing that the weight of their resentment might come storming down on him from the peak of their Babylonian grandeur, as though from lofty cedars on Lebanon not yet felled by the Lord.[25] But later he drank in courage from his avid reading and came to fear that he might be disowned by Christ before his holy angels if he feared to confess him before men and women.[26] In his own eyes he was guilty of a great crime in being ashamed of the holy mysteries instituted by your humble Word, while feeling no shame at the sacrilegious rites of proud demons, whose likeness he had been proud to assume himself. Accordingly he threw off the shamefacedness provoked by vanity and became modest in the face of truth: suddenly and without warning he said to Simplicianus, who told this tale, "Let us go to church: I want to become a Christian."

Hardly able to contain his joy, Simplicianus went with him. He was initiated into the first stage of the catechumenate, and not long afterward he gave in his name, asking for rebirth in baptism. Rome stood amazed, while the Church was jubilant. The proud looked on and fumed with anger; they ground their teeth in impotent fury[27]; but as for your

---

25. See Ps 28 (29):15.
26. See Mk 8:38 and par.
27. See Ps 111 (112):10.

servant, the Lord God was his hope, and he had no eyes for vanities or lying follies.[28]

5. Eventually the time came for him to make his profession of faith. Custom decrees that those who are approaching your grace in baptism make their profession in the presence of the baptized community of Rome, standing on a raised platform and using a set form of words which has been entrusted to them and committed to memory. Simplicianus told me that Victorious had been offered by the priests the option of making his statement more privately, for it was customary to offer this concession to people who were likely to lose their nerve through shyness, but that he had chosen rather to proclaim his salvation before the holy company. What he taught in rhetoric was not salvation, he said, yet he had professed that publicly enough. If he was not afraid to address crowds of crazy people in his own words, how much less ought he to fear your peaceable flock as he uttered your Word?

As he climbed up to repeat the Creed they all shouted his name to one another in a clamorous outburst of thanksgiving—everyone who knew him, that is, and was there anyone present who did not? Then in more subdued tones the word passed from joyful mouth to joyful mouth among them all: "Victorinus, Victorinus!" Spontaneous was their shout of delight as they saw him, and spontaneous their attentive silence to hear him. With magnificent confidence he proclaimed the

---

28. See Ps 39:5 (40:4).

true faith, and all the people longed to clasp him tenderly to their hearts. And so they did, by loving him and rejoicing with him, for those affections were like clasping hands.

3, 6. O God, who are so good, what is it in the human heart that makes us rejoice more intensely over the salvation of a soul which is despaired of but then freed from grave danger, than we would if there had always been good prospects for it and its peril slighter? You too, merciful Father, yes, even you are more joyful over one repentant sinner than over ninety-nine righteous people who need no repentance.[29] And we likewise listen with overflowing gladness when we hear how the shepherd carries back on exultant shoulders the sheep that had strayed,[30] and how the coin is returned to your treasury as neighbors share the glee of the woman who found it,[31] while the joy of your eucharistic assembly wrings tears from us when the story is read in your house of a younger son who *was dead, but has come back to life, was lost but is found.*[32] You express your own joy through ours, and through the joy of your angels who are made holy by their holy charity; for you yourself are ever the same,[33] and all transient things, things which cannot abide constantly in their mode of being, are known to your unchanging intelligence.

7. What is going on in our minds, then, that we should

---

29. See Lk 15:4–7.
30. See Lk 15:4–6; Ps 118 (119): 176.
31. See Lk 15:8–9.
32. Lk 15:24—32.
33. See Ps 101:28 (102:27).

be more highly delighted at finding cherished objects, or having them restored to us, than if we had always kept them safe? Other instances bear this out, and all our experience shouts its corroboration, "Yes, truly this is so." A victorious emperor celebrates his triumph. He would not have been victorious had there been no war, and the more imperiled he has been in battle, the more elated he is in his triumph.

Or a storm batters mariners and threatens them with shipwreck. Every face pales at the prospect of death, but sky and sea grow calm, and the sailors' joy is as intense as lately was their fear. Or someone we love falls sick. His pulse betrays the gravity of his condition, and all who long for his recovery are equally tormented in their minds. Then he takes a turn for the better, and although he is not yet walking with his pristine vigor there is already such joy as never there was when in earlier days he strode about well and strong.

Even the natural pleasures of human life are attained through distress, not only through the unexpected calamities that befall against our will but also through deliberate and planned discomfort. There is no pleasure in eating and drinking unless the discomfort of hunger and thirst have preceded them. Drunkards eat somewhat salty food to induce a searing, parched sensation, which will be deliciously quenched by a drink. Then again, custom requires that after betrothal brides shall not be handed over immediately, lest after marriage a man hold cheap the woman for whom he did not as a bridegroom have to sigh and wait.

8. This law holds for shameful, demeaning pleasure, but the same is true for what is permitted and lawful, the same for the most sincere and honorable friendship, and the same for that young man who had died but come back to life, had perished but was found. In every case greater sorrow issues in greater joy. How can this be, O Lord my God, when you are yourself your own eternal joy, and all around you heaven rejoices in you eternally? Why is it that our part of creation swings between decay and growth, pain and reconciliation? Perhaps because this is the proper mode of being for these things and with this alone you endowed them when from highest heaven to the lowest places of the earth, from the dawn of the ages to their end, from angel to tiny worm, from the first stirring of change to the last, you assigned all classes of good things and all your righteous works to their appropriate places, and activated them at their proper times?

Ah, how high you are in the heights of heaven,[34] how deep in the depths! From no place are you absent, yet how tardily do we return to you!

4, 9. Come, Lord, arouse us and call us back, kindle us and seize us, prove to us how sweet you are in your burning tenderness; let us love you and run to you.[35] Are there not many who return to you from a deeper, blinder pit than did Victorious, many who draw near to you and are illumined[36]

34. See Ps 112 (113):4–5; Is 33:5.
35. See Sg 1:2–3.
36. See Ps 33:6 (34:5).

as they welcome the light, and in welcoming it receive from you the power to become children of God?[37] Yet if they are less well known to the populace, even people who do know them find less joy in their conversion, because whenever joy is shared among many, even the gladness of individuals is increased, for all are affected by the common enthusiasm and they catch the flame from one another. Moreover, the fact that these converts are generally known ensures that they become for many an authoritative example pointing toward salvation; they forge ahead of crowds that will follow. That is why many who have made the journey before them rejoice particularly, with an eye to others besides these lone individuals.

Forbid it, Lord, that rich personages should ever be more welcome in your tabernacle than the poor, or the nobility than lowly folk,[38] when your own preferential choice fell upon the weak things of this world in order to shame the strong, upon lowly things, contemptible things and nonentities, as though they really were, to set at nought the things that are.[39] Nevertheless the least of your apostles,[40] through whose tongue you sent those words re-echoing, loved to be called not by his former name, "Saul," but "Paul," to commemorate that glorious victory when the proconsul Paulus,[41] his pride beaten down by the apostle's arms, was brought under Christ's lenient yoke

37. See Jn 1:9, 12.
38. See Dt 1:17; 16:19; Sir 42:1; Acts 10:34; Jas 2:1–9.
39. See 1 Cor 1:27–28; Rom 4:17.
40. See 1 Cor 15:9.
41. See Acts 13:7–12.

to become a common subject of the great King. The enemy is more thoroughly trounced in a person over whom he had a more powerful hold, or through whom he had a hold over a greater number of others; and stronger is his grip over those who on pretext of nobility are proud, stronger too his hold over many another on pretext of their authority.

The higher, then, the value set on the soul of Victorious, which the devil had captured as an impregnable stronghold, and on Victorinus' tongue, which the devil had wielded like a huge, sharp weapon to destroy many, the greater was the gladness with which your children rightly rejoiced on seeing the powerful foe bound by our King[42] and his weaponry seized, cleaned, and made fit to serve in your honor as equipment useful to the Master for every good purpose.[43]

Augustine longs to imitate him, but is hindered by lustful habit

5, 10. On hearing this story I was fired to imitate Victorious; indeed it was to this end that your servant Simplicianus had related it. But he added a further point. When in the reign of the Emperor Julian a law was passed which forbade Christians to teach literature and rhetoric, Victorious willingly complied, for he preferred to abandon his school of

42. See Mt 12:29.
43. See 2 Tm 2:21.

talkativeness rather than forsake your word, through which you impart eloquence to the tongues of speechless babes.[44] In my eyes he appeared not so much heroic as all the happier for having taken this step, since it afforded him the opportunity to be at leisure for you. I ached for a like chance myself, for it was no iron chain imposed by anyone else that fettered me, but the iron of my own will. The enemy had my power of willing in his clutches, and from it had forged a chain to bind me. The truth is that disordered lust springs from a perverted will; when lust is pandered to, a habit is formed; when habit is not checked, it hardens into compulsion. These were like interlinking rings forming what I have described as a chain, and my harsh servitude used it to keep me under duress.

A new will had begun to emerge in me, the will to worship you disinterestedly[45] and enjoy you, O God, our only sure felicity; but it was not yet capable of surmounting that earlier will strengthened by inveterate custom. And so the two wills fought it out—the old and the new,[46] the one carnal, the other spiritual—and in their struggle tore my soul apart.

11. I thus came to understand from my own experience what I had read, how the flesh lusts against the spirit and the spirit strives against the flesh.[47] I was aligned with both,

44. See Wis 10:21.
45. See Jb 1:9.
46. See Eph 4:22–24; Col 3:9–10.
47. See Gal 5:17.

but more with the desires I approved in myself than with those I frowned upon, for in these latter I was not really the agent, since for the most part I was enduring them against my will rather than acting freely.[48] All the same, the force of habit that fought against me had grown fiercer by my own doing, because I had come willingly to this point where I now wished not to be. And who has any right to object, when just punishment catches up with a sinner?

I had grown used to pretending that the only reason why I had not yet turned my back on the world to serve you was that my perception of the truth was uncertain, but that excuse was no longer available to me, for by now it was certain. But I was still entangled by the earth and refused to enlist in your service,[49] for the prospect of being freed from all these encumbrances frightened me as much as the encumbrances themselves ought to have done.

12. I was thus weighed down by the pleasant burden of the world in the way one commonly is by sleep, and the thoughts with which I attempted to meditate upon you[50] were like the efforts of people who are trying to wake up, but are overpowered and immersed once more in slumberous deeps. No one wants to be asleep all the time, and it is generally agreed among sensible people that being awake is a better state, yet it often happens that a person puts off the moment when he

48. See Ps 62:7 (63:6).
49. See 2 Tm 2:4.
50. See Rom 7:16–17.

must shake himself out of sleep because his limbs are heavy with a lassitude that pulls him toward the more attractive alternative, even though he is already trying to resist it and the hour for rising has come; in a similar way I was quite sure that surrendering myself to your love would be better than succumbing to my lust, but while the former course commended itself and was beginning to conquer, the latter charmed and chained me. I had no answer to give as you said to me, *Arise, sleeper, rise from the dead: Christ will enlighten you,*[51] and plied me with evidence that you spoke truly; no, I was convinced by the truth and had no answer whatever except the sluggish, drowsy words, "Just a minute," "One more minute," "Let me have a little longer." But these "minutes" never diminished, and my "little longer" lasted inordinately long.

To find my delight in your law as far as my inmost self was concerned was of no profit to me when a different law in my bodily members was warring against the law of my mind imprisoning me under the law of sin which held sway in my lower self. For the law of sin is that brute force of habit whereby the mind is dragged along and held fast against its will, and deservedly so because it slipped into the habit willingly. In my wretched state, who was there to free me from this death-doomed body, save your grace through Jesus Christ our Lord?[52]

51. Eph 5:14.
52. See Rom 7:24–25.

Conversation with Ponticianus

6, 13. Now I will relate how you set me free from a craving for sexual gratification which fettered me like a tight-drawn chain, and from my enslavement to worldly affairs: I will confess to your name, O Lord,[53] my helper and redeemer.

I continued to attend to my accustomed duties, but with mounting anxiety. I longed for you every day and spent as much time in your church as could be spared from my business, under the weight of which I was groaning. With me was Alypius, who since his third stint as assessor[54] had been without legal advisory work, and was now looking round for clients to whom he might once more sell his counsel, just as I was trying to sell the art of speaking, insofar as it ever can be imparted by teaching. Nebridius, however, yielding to our friendly persuasion, had consented to act as assistant teacher to Verecundus, a citizen and schoolmaster of Milan who was very well known to us all. This man had most earnestly desired reliable help from someone of our company, for he stood in sore need of it, and he had reinforced his insistent plea by appealing to his close association with us. Nebridius was not, therefore, attracted to this post by ambition for the advantages it might bring him, for he could have done better by the profession of literature, had he willed; he undertook it simply as a kindly service because, being such a very

---

53. See Ps 53:8 (54:6).
54. See VI, 10, 16.

gentle and accommodating friend, he was unwilling to set our request aside. He carried out his duties with the utmost discretion, taking care not to attract the attention of persons whom the world regarded as important. He thus steered clear of any mental disturbance they might have caused him, for he wanted to keep his mind free and disengaged for as much of his time as he possibly could, with a view to research and to reading or listening to anything connected with wisdom.

14. On a certain day when Nebridius was absent (I forget why), something happened. A man named Ponticianus, who held an important post at court, came to our house to visit Alypius and me; being an African he was our compatriot, and he wanted something or other from us. We sat down together and talked. His eye happened to light upon a book that lay on a gaming table nearby; he picked it up, opened it and found it to be the letters of the apostle Paul. This was certainly unexpected, for he had supposed it to be the kind of thing I exhausted myself in teaching. But then he smiled, looked up at me and offered his congratulations, surprised by his sudden discovery that those writings, and those alone, were under my eye. He was himself a baptized Christian and made a practice of prostrating himself in church before you, our God, in frequent and prolonged prayers. When I remarked that I was applying myself to intensive study of those scriptures, he began to tell us about the monk Antony of Egypt, whose name was illustrious and held in high honor among your servants, though we had never heard it until this moment. When

Ponticianus learned this he dwelt more fully on the subject, enlightening us about the great man; he was astonished at our ignorance. But we were stupefied as we listened to the tale of the wonders you had worked within the true faith of the Catholic Church, especially as they were most firmly attested by recent memory and had occurred so near to our own times. So all of us were amazed: we because they were so tremendous, and he because we had never heard of them.

15. His discourse led on from this topic to the proliferation of monasteries, the sweet fragrance rising up to you from the lives of monks, and the fecund wastelands of the desert. We had known nothing of all this. There was even a monastery full of good brothers at Milan, outside the city walls, under Ambrose's care, yet we were unaware of it.

Story of conversion of two court officials at Trier

Ponticianus went on talking and developing the theme, while we listened, spellbound. So it came about that he told us that one day when the court was at Trier he and three of his colleagues went out for a walk in the gardens abutting on the walls, while the emperor was occupied with the morning show at the circus. Now it happened that as they strolled about they split into pairs, one companion staying with Ponticianus while the other two went off by themselves. In their wandering these latter chanced upon a cottage where some servants of yours were living, men poor in spirit, the kind of people to whom the kingdom of heaven belongs.[55] There they found a book which contained *The Life of Antony*. One of them began to read it. His admiration and enthusiasm were aroused, and as he read he began to mull over the possibility of appropriating the same kind of life for himself, by renouncing his secular career to serve you alone. (He belonged to the ranks of so-called administrative officers.) Then quite suddenly he was filled with a love of holiness and a realistic sense of shame and disgust with himself[56]; he turned his gaze toward his friend and demanded, "Tell me: where do we hope all our efforts are going to get us? What are we looking for? In whose cause are we striving? Does life at court promise us anything better than promotion to being Friends of the Emperor? And once we are, will that not be a precarious position, fraught with perils? Will it not mean negotiating many a hazard, only to end in greater danger still? And how long would it take us to get there? Whereas I can become a friend of God[57] here and now if I want to."

Even as he spoke he was in labor with the new life that was struggling to birth within him. He directed his eyes back to the page, and as he read a change began to occur in that hidden place within him where you alone can see; his mind was being stripped of the world, as presently became apparent. The flood tide of his heart leapt on, and at last he broke

---

55. See Mt 5:3.
56. See Ps 4:5 (4).
57. See Jas 2:23; Jdt 8:22.

off his reading with a groan as he discerned the right course and determined to take it. By now he belonged to you. "I have already torn myself away from the ambitions we cherished, and have made up my mind to serve God," he told his friend. "I am going to set about it this very moment and in this place. If you have no stomach to imitate me, at least don't stand in my way." The other replied that he would bear him company, both in the noble reward and in the glorious combat. And both of them, now enlisted in your service, began to build their tower, knowing the cost full well: they abandoned all their possessions and followed you.[58]

Meanwhile Ponticianus was walking with his companion through other parts of the garden. In search of their friends they arrived at the place, and on finding them there urged them to return, for it was growing late. They, however, told their story, announcing the plan on which they had resolved and describing how the will to take this course had arisen within them and grown firm; and they begged their friends at least to place no obstacles in their way, if they had no mind to join them. Ponticianus and his companion shed tears on their own account, as he related, even though they were in no way altered from the men they had been. They offered devout congratulations to their friends and commended themselves to their prayers; then they went back to the palace, dragging heavy hearts along the ground, while their friends stayed in

58.   See Lk 14:28; Mt 19:27; Lk 5:11, 28.

the cottage with hearts set on heaven. Both were engaged to be married, and when their fiancées later heard of their decision, they likewise dedicated their virginity to you.

7, 16. Ponticianus went on with his story; but, Lord, even while he spoke you were wrenching me back toward myself, and pulling me round from that standpoint behind my back[59] which I had taken to avoid looking at myself. You set me down before my face,[60] forcing me to mark how despicable I was, how misshapen and begrimed, filthy and festering. I saw and shuddered. If I tried to turn my gaze away, he went on relentlessly telling his tale, and you set me before myself once more, thrusting me into my sight that I might perceive my sin and hate it.[61] I had been aware of it all along, but I had been glossing over it, suppressing it and forgetting.

17. But now self-abhorrence possessed me, all the harsher as my heart went out more ardently to those young men, and I heard of the blessed impulsiveness with which they had without reserve handed themselves over to you for healing. By contrast with them I felt myself loathsome, remembering how many of my years—twelve, perhaps—had gone to waste, and I with them, since my nineteenth year when I was aroused to pursue wisdom by the reading of Cicero's *Hortensius*. I had been putting off the moment when by spurning earthly happiness I would clear space in my life to search for

59. See Jer 2:27.
60. See Ps 49 (50):21.
61. See Ps 35:3 (36:2).

wisdom; yet even to seek it, let alone find it, would have been more rewarding than discovery of treasure or possession of all this world's kingdoms, or having every bodily pleasure at my beck and call. I had been extremely miserable in adolescence, miserable from its very onset, and as I prayed to you for the gift of chastity I had even pleaded, "Grant me chastity and self-control, but please not yet." I was afraid that you might hear me immediately and heal me forthwith of the morbid lust which I was more anxious to satisfy than to snuff out. So I had wandered off into the crooked paths[62] of a sacrilegious superstition, not because I had any certainty about it but because I preferred it to other beliefs—not that I was investigating these in any spirit of reverence: rather was I opposing them with malicious intent.

18. I had been telling myself that my reason for putting off day after day[63] the decision to renounce worldly ambition and follow you alone was that I could as yet see no certain light by which to steer my course. But the day had dawned when I was stripped naked in my own eyes and my conscience challenged me within: "Where is your ready tongue now? You have been professing yourself reluctant to throw off your load of illusion because truth was uncertain. Well, it is certain now, yet the burden still weighs you down, while other people are given wings on freer shoulders,[64] people who have not worn

---

62. See Sir 2:16.
63. See Sir 5:8.
64. See Ps 54:7 (55:6).

themselves out with research, nor spent a decade and more reflecting on these questions."

My conscience gnawed away at me in this fashion, and I was fiercely shamed and flung into hideous confusion while Ponticianus was relating all this. Having brought the conversation to a close and settled his business with us, he returned to his place, and I to myself.

Was anything left unsaid in my inner debate? Was there any whip of sage advice I left unused to lash my soul into coming with me, as I tried to follow you? It fought and resisted, but could find no excuse. All its arguments had been used up and refuted, but there remained a dumb dread: frightful as death seemed the restraining of habit's oozy discharge, that very seepage which was rotting it to death.

Struggle in the garden

8, 19. Within the house of my spirit the violent conflict raged on, the quarrel with my soul that I had so powerfully provoked in our secret dwelling, my heart,[65] and at the height of it I rushed to Alypius with my mental anguish plain upon my face. "What is happening to us?" I exclaimed. "What does this mean? What did you make of it? The untaught are rising up and taking heaven by storm,[66] while we with all our dreary

---

65. See Mt 11:12.
66. See Mt 6:6.

teachings are still groveling in this world of flesh and blood![67]
Are we ashamed to follow, just because they have taken the
lead, yet not ashamed of lacking the courage even to follow?"
Some such words as these I spoke, and then my frenzy tore me
away from him, while he regarded me in silent bewilderment.
Unusual, certainly, was my speech, but my brow, cheeks and
eyes, my flushed countenance and the cadences of my voice
expressed my mind more fully than the words I uttered.

Adjacent to our lodgings was a small garden. We were free
to make use of it as well as of the house, for our host, who
owned the house, did not live there. The tumult in my breast
had swept me away to this place, where no one would inter-
fere with the blazing dispute I had engaged in with myself
until it should be resolved. What the outcome would be you
knew, not I. All I knew was that I was going mad, but for
the sake of my sanity, and dying that I might live, aware of
the evil that I was but unaware of the good I was soon to
become. So I went out into the garden and Alypius followed
at my heels; my privacy was not infringed by his presence,
and, in any case, how could he abandon me in that state? We
sat down as far as possible from the house. I was groaning in
spirit[68] and shaken by violent anger because I could form no
resolve to enter into a covenant with you, though in my bones
I knew that this was what I ought to do,[69] and everything in

---

67. See 1 Cor 15:50; Mt 16:17; Gal 1:16.
68. See Jn 11:33.
69. See I, 18, 28.

me lauded such a course to the skies. It was a journey not to be undertaken by ship or carriage or on foot[70] nor need it take me even that short distance I had walked from the house to the place where we were sitting; for to travel—and more, to reach journey's end—was nothing else but to want to go there, but to want it valiantly and with all my heart, not to whirl and toss this way and that a will half crippled by the struggle, as part of it rose up to walk while part sank down.

20. While this vacillation was at its most intense many of my bodily gestures were of the kind that people sometimes want to perform but cannot, either because the requisite limbs are missing, or because they are bound and restricted, or paralyzed through illness, or in some other way impeded. If I tore out my hair, battered my forehead, entwined my fingers and clasped them round my knee, I did so because I wanted to. I might have wanted to but found myself unable, if my limbs had not been mobile enough to obey. So then, there were plenty of actions that I performed where willing was not the same thing as being able; yet I was not doing the one thing that was incomparably more desirable to me, the thing that I would be able to do as soon as I willed, because as soon as I willed—why, then, I would be willing it! For in this sole instance the faculty to act and the will to act precisely coincide, and the willing is already the doing. Yet this was not happening. My body was more ready to obey the slightest

---

70. See Ps 34 (35):10.

whim of my soul in the matter of moving my limbs, than the soul was to obey its own command in carrying out this major volition, which was to be accomplished within the will alone.

9, 21. How did this bizarre situation arise, how develop? May your mercy shed light on my inquiry, so that perhaps an answer may be found in the mysterious punishments meted out to humankind, those utterly baffling pains that afflict the children of Adam. How then did this bizarre situation arise, how develop? The mind commands the body and is instantly obeyed; the mind commands itself, and meets with resistance. When the mind orders the hand to move, so smooth is the compliance that command can scarcely be distinguished from execution; yet the mind is mind, while the hand is body. When the mind issues its command that the mind itself should will something (and the mind so commanded is no other than itself), it fails to do so. How did this bizarre situation arise, how develop? As I say, the mind commands itself to will something: it would not be giving the order if it did not want this thing; yet it does not do what it commands.

Evidently, then, it does not want this thing with the whole of itself, and therefore the command does not proceed from an undivided mind. Inasmuch as it issues the command, it does will it, but inasmuch as the command is not carried out, it does not will it. What the will is ordering is that a certain volition should exist, and this volition is not some alien thing, but its very self. Hence it cannot be giving the order with its whole self. It cannot be identical with that thing which it is commanding to come into existence, for if it were whole and entire it would not command itself to be, since it would be already.

This partial willing and partial non-willing is thus not so bizarre, but a sickness of the mind, which cannot rise with its whole self on the wings of truth because it is heavily burdened by habit. There are two wills, then, and neither is the whole: what one has the other lacks.

10, 22. Some there are who on perceiving two wills engaged in deliberation assert that in us there are two natures, one good, the other evil, each with a mind of its own. Let them perish from your presence, O God,[71] as perish all who talk wildly and lead our minds astray.[72] They are evil themselves as long as they hold these opinions, yet these same people will be good if they embrace true opinions and assent to true teaching, and so merit the apostle's commendation, *You were darkness once, but now you are light in the Lord.*[73] The trouble is that they want to be light not in the Lord but in themselves, with their notion that the soul is by nature divine, and so they have become denser darkness still, because by their appalling arrogance they have moved further away from you, the true Light, who enlighten everyone who comes into the world.[74] I warn these people, Take stock of what you are saying, and let

---

71. See Ps 67:3 (68:2).
72. See Ti 1:10.
73. Eph 5:8.
74. See Jn 1:9.

it shame you; but once draw near to him and be illumined, and your faces will not blush with shame.[75] When I was making up my mind to serve the Lord my God[76] at last, as I had long since purposed, I was the one who wanted to follow that course, and I was the one who wanted not to. I was the only one involved. I neither wanted it wholeheartedly nor turned from it wholeheartedly. I was at odds with myself, and fragmenting myself. This disintegration was occurring without my consent, but what it indicated was not the presence in me of a mind belonging to some alien nature but the punishment undergone by my own. In this sense, and this sense only, it was not I who brought it about, but the sin that dwelt within me[77] as penalty for that other sin committed with greater freedom; for I was a son of Adam.

23. Moreover, if we were to take the number of conflicting urges to signify the number of natures present in us, we should have to assume that there are not two, but many. If someone is trying to make up his mind whether to go to a Manichean conventicle or to the theater, the Manichees declare, "There you are, there's the evidence for two natures: the good one is dragging him our way, the bad one is pulling him back in the other direction. How else explain this dithering between contradictory wills?" But I regard both as bad, the one that leads him to them and the one that lures

75. See Ps 33:6 (34:5).
76. See Dt 6:13; Mt 4:10; Jer 30:9.
77. See Rom 7:17, 20.

him back to the theater. They, on the contrary, think that an inclination toward them can only be good.

But consider this: suppose one of our people is deliberating, and as two desires clash he is undecided whether to go to the theater or to our church, will not our opponents too be undecided what attitude to take? Either they will have to admit that it is good will that leads a person to our church, just as good as that which leads to theirs the people who are initiated into their sacred rites and trapped there—and this they are unwilling to admit; or they will conclude that two evil natures and two bad minds are pitted against each other within one person, in which case their habitual assertion of one good and one evil nature will be erroneous; or, finally, they will be brought round to the truth and no longer deny that when a person is deliberating there is but one soul, thrown into turmoil by divergent impulses.

24. When, therefore, they observe two conflicting impulses within one person, let them stop saying that two hostile minds are at war, one good, the other evil, and that these derive from two hostile substances and two hostile principles. For you are true, O God, and so you chide and rebuke them and prove them wrong. The choice may lie between two impulses that are both evil, as when a person is debating whether to murder someone with poison or a dagger; whether to annex this part of another man's property or that, assuming he cannot get both; whether to buy himself pleasure by extravagant spending or hoard his money out of avarice; whether to go to

the circus or the theater if both performances are on the same day—and I would even add a third possibility: whether to go and steal from someone else's house while he has the chance, and a fourth as well: whether to commit adultery while he is about it. All these impulses may occur together, at exactly the same time, and all be equally tempting, but they cannot all be acted upon at once. The mind is then rent apart by the plethora of desirable objects as four inclinations, or even more, do battle among themselves; yet the Manichees do not claim that there are as many disparate substances in us as this.

The same holds true for good impulses. I would put these questions to them: Is it good to find delight in a reading from the apostle? To enjoy the serenity of a psalm? To discuss the gospel? To each point they will reply, "Yes, that is good." Where does that leave us? If all these things tug at our will with equal force, and all together at the same time, will not these divergent inclinations put a great strain on the human heart, as we deliberate which to select? All are good, but they compete among themselves until one is chosen, to which the will, hitherto distracted between many options, may move as a united whole. So too when the joys of eternity call us from above, and pleasure in temporal prosperity holds us fast below, our one soul is in no state to embrace either with its entire will. Claimed by truth for the one, to the other clamped by custom, the soul is torn apart in its distress.

11, 25. Such was the sickness in which I agonized, blaming myself more sharply than ever, turning and twisting in my chain as I strove to tear free from it completely, for slender indeed was the bond that still held me. But hold me it did. In my secret heart you stood by me, Lord, redoubling the lashes of fear and shame in the severity of your mercy, lest I give up the struggle and that slender, fragile bond that remained be not broken after all, but thicken again and constrict me more tightly. "Let it be now," I was saying to myself. "Now is the moment, let it be now," and merely by saying this I was moving toward the decision. I would almost achieve it, but then fall just short; yet I did not slip right down to my starting-point, but stood aside to get my breath back. Then I would make a fresh attempt, and now I was almost there, almost there...I was touching the goal, grasping it...and then I was not there, not touching, not grasping it. I shrank from dying to death and living to life, for ingrained evil was more powerful in me than new-grafted good.

The nearer it came, that moment when I would be changed, the more it pierced me with terror. Dismayed, but not quite dislodged, I was left hanging.

26. The frivolity of frivolous aims, the futility of futile pursuits,[78] these things that had been my cronies of long standing, still held me back, plucking softly at my garment of flesh and murmuring in my ear, "Do you mean to get rid of us? Shall we never be your companions again after that moment... never...never again? From that time onward so-and-so will be

---

78.   See Eccl 1:2; 12:8.

forbidden to you, all your life long." And what was it that they were reminding me of by those words, "so-and-so," O my God, what were they bringing to my mind? May your mercy banish such memories far from me! What foul deeds were they not hinting at, what disgraceful exploits! But now their voices were less than half as loud, for they no longer confronted me directly to argue their case, but muttered behind my back and slyly tweaked me as I walked away, trying to make me look back. Yet they did slow me down, for I could not bring myself to tear free and shake them off and leap across to that place whither I was summoned, while aggressive habit still taunted me: "Do you imagine you will be able to live without these things?"

27. The taunts had begun to sound much less persuasive, however; for a revelation was coming to me from that country toward which I was facing, but into which I trembled to cross. There I beheld the chaste, dignified figure of Continence. Calm and cheerful was her manner, though modest, pure and honorable her charm as she coaxed me to come and hesitate no longer, stretching kindly hands to welcome and embrace me, hands filled with a wealth of heartening examples. A multitude of boys and girls were there, a great concourse of youth and persons of every age, venerable widows and women grown old in their virginity, and in all of them I saw that this same Continence was by no means sterile, but the fruitful mother of children[79] conceived in joy from you,

---

79. See Ps 112 (113):9.

her Bridegroom. She was smiling at me, but with a challenging smile, as though to say, "Can you not do what these men have done, these women? Could any of them achieve it by their own strength, without the Lord their God? He it was, the Lord their God, who granted me to them. Why try to stand by yourself, only to lose your footing? Cast yourself on him and do not be afraid: he will not step back and let you fall. Cast yourself upon him trustfully; he will support and heal you." And I was bitterly ashamed, because I could still hear the murmurs of those frivolities, and I was still in suspense, still hanging back. Again she appealed to me, as though urging, "Close your ears against those unclean parts of you which belong to the earth[80] and let them be put to death. They tell you titillating tales, but have nothing to do with the law of the Lord your God."[81] All this argument in my heart raged only between myself and myself. Alypius stood fast at my side, silently awaiting the outcome of my unprecedented agitation.

12, 28. But as this deep meditation dredged all my wretchedness up from the secret profundity of my being and heaped it all together before the eyes of my heart, a huge storm blew up within me and brought on a heavy rain of tears. In order to pour them out unchecked with the sobs that accompanied them I arose and left Alypius, for solitude

---

80. See Col 3:5.
81. See Ps 118 (119):85.

seemed to me more suitable for the business of weeping. I withdrew far enough to ensure that his presence—even his—would not be burdensome to me. This was my need, and he understood it, for I think I had risen to my feet and blurted out something, my voice already choked with tears. He accordingly remained, in stunned amazement, at the place where we had been sitting. I flung myself down somehow under a fig-tree and gave free rein to the tears that burst from my eyes like rivers, as an acceptable sacrifice to you.[82] Many things I had to say to you, and the gist of them, though not the precise words, was: "O Lord, how long?[83] How long? Will you be angry for ever? Do not remember our age-old sins."[84] For by these I was conscious of being held prisoner. I uttered cries of misery: "Why must I go on saying, 'Tomorrow…tomorrow'? Why not now? Why not put an end to my depravity this very hour?"

"Pick it up and read"

29. I went on talking like this and weeping in the intense bitterness of my broken heart.[85] Suddenly I heard a voice from a house nearby—perhaps a voice of some boy or girl, I do not know—singing over and over again, "Pick it up and read,

---

82. See Ps 50:19 (51:17).
83. See Ps 6:4 (3).
84. See Ps 78 (79):5, 8.
85. See Ps 50:19 (51:17).

pick it up and read." My expression immediately altered and I began to think hard whether children ordinarily repeated a ditty like this in any sort of game, but I could not recall ever having heard it anywhere else. I stemmed the flood of tears and rose to my feet, believing that this could be nothing other than a divine command to open the Book and read the first passage I chanced upon; for I had heard the story of how Antony had been instructed by a gospel text. He happened to arrive while the gospel was being read, and took the words to be addressed to himself when he heard, *Go and sell all you possess and give the money to the poor: you will have treasure in heaven. Then come, follow me.*[86] So he was promptly converted to you by this plainly divine message. Stung into action, I returned to the place where Alypius was sitting, for on leaving it I had put down there the book of the apostle's letters. I snatched it up, opened it and read in silence the passage on which my eyes first lighted: *Not in dissipation and drunkenness, nor in debauchery and lewdness, nor in arguing and jealousy; but put on the Lord Jesus Christ, and make no provision for the flesh or the gratification of your desires.*[87] I had no wish to read further, nor was there need. No sooner had I reached the end of the verse than the light of certainty flooded my heart and all dark shades of doubt fled away.

---

86. Mt 19:21.
87. Rom 13:13–14.

Conversion of Augustine and Alypius; Monica's joy

30. I closed the book, marking the place with a finger between the leaves or by some other means, and told Alypius what had happened. My face was peaceful now. He in return told me what had been happening to him without my knowledge. He asked to see what I had read: I showed him, but he looked further than my reading had taken me. I did not know what followed, but the next verse was, *Make room for the person who is weak in faith.*[88] He referred this text to himself and interpreted it to me. Confirmed by this admonition he associated himself with my decision and good purpose without any upheaval or delay, for it was entirely in harmony with his own moral character, which for a long time now had been far, far better than mine.

We went indoors and told my mother, who was overjoyed. When we related to her how it had happened she was filled with triumphant delight and blessed you, who have power to do more than we ask or understand,[89] for she saw that you had granted her much more in my regard than she had been wont to beg of you in her wretched, tearful groaning. Many years earlier you had shown her a vision of me standing on the rule of faith[90]; and now indeed I stood there, no longer seeking a wife or entertaining any worldly hope, for you had

---

88. Rom 14:1.
89. See Eph 3:10.
90. See III, 11,19.

converted me to yourself. In so doing you had also converted her grief into a joy[91] far more abundant than she had desired, and much more tender and chaste than she could ever have looked to find in grandchildren from my flesh.

---

91. See Ps 29:12 (30:11).

notes

notes

Letter to His Children's Tutor, William Gunnell (MAY 22, 1518?)

ST. THOMAS MORE

I have received, my dear Gunnell, your letter, elegant, as your letters always are, and full of affection. From your letter I perceive your devotion to my children; I argue their diligence from their own. Every one of their letters pleased me, but I was particularly pleased, because I notice that Elizabeth shows a gentleness and self-command in the absence of her mother, which some children would not show in her presence. Let her understand that such conduct delights me more than all possible letters I could receive from anyone. Though I prefer learning joined with virtue to all the treasures of kings, yet renown for learning, when it is not united with a good life, is nothing else than splendid and notorious infamy: this would be specially the case in a woman.

Since erudition in women is a new thing and a reproach to the sloth of men, many will gladly assail it, and impute to literature what is really the fault of nature, thinking from the vices of the learned to get their own ignorance esteemed as virtue. On the other hand, if a woman (and this I desire and hope with you as their teacher for all my daughters) to eminent virtue should add an outwork of even moderate skill in literature, I think she will have more real profit than if she had obtained the riches of Croesus and the beauty of Helen. I do not say this because of the glory which will be hers, though glory follows virtue as a shadow follows a body, but because the reward of wisdom is too solid to be lost like riches or to decay like beauty, since it depends on the intimate conscience of what is right, not on the talk of men, than which nothing is more foolish or mischievous.

It belongs to a good man, no doubt, to avoid infamy, but to lay himself out for renown is the conduct of a man who is not only proud, but ridiculous and miserable. A soul must be without peace which is ever fluctuating between elation and disappointment from the opinions of men. Among all the benefits that learning bestows on men, there is none more excellent than this, that by the study of books we are taught in that very study to seek not praise, but utility.

Such has been the teaching of the most learned men, especially of philosophers, who are the guides of human life, although some may have abused learning, like other good things, simply to 30 court empty glory and popular renown. I have dwelt so much on this matter, my dear Gunnell, because of what you say in your letter, that Margaret's lofty character should not be abased. In this judgment I quite agree with you; but to me, and, no doubt, to you also, that man would seem to abase a generous character who should accustom it to admire what is vain and low. He, on the contrary, raises the character who rises to virtue and true goods, and who looks down with contempt from the contemplation of what is sublime, on those shadows of good things which almost all mortals, through ignorance of truth, greedily snatch at as if they were true goods.

Therefore, my dear Gunnell, since we must walk by this road, I have often begged not you only, who, out of your affection for my children, would do it of your own accord, nor my wife, who is sufficiently urged by her maternal love for them, which has been proved to me in so many ways, but all my friends, to warn my children to avoid the precipices of pride and haughtiness, and to walk in the pleasant meadows of modesty; not to be dazzled at the sight of gold; not to lament that they do not possess what they erroneously admire in others; not to think more of themselves for gaudy trappings, nor less for the want of them; neither to deform the beauty that nature has given them by neglect, nor to try to heighten it by artifice; to put virtue in the first place, learning in the second; and in their studies to esteem most whatever may teach them piety towards God, charity to all, and modesty and Christian humility in themselves. By such means they will receive from God the reward of an innocent life, and in the assured expectation of it, will view death without horror, and meanwhile possessing solid joy, will neither be puffed up by the empty praise of men, nor dejected by evil tongues. These I consider the genuine fruits of learning, and though I admit that all literary men do not possess them, I would maintain that those who give themselves to study with such views, will easily attain their end and become perfect.

Nor do I think that the harvest will be much affected whether it is a man or a woman who sows the field. They both have the same human nature, which reason differentiates from that of beasts; both, therefore, are equally suited for those studies by which reason is cultivated, and becomes fruitful like a ploughed land on which the seed of good lessons has been sown. If it be true that the soil of woman's brain be bad, and apter to bear bracken than corn, by which saying many keep women from study, I think, on the contrary, that a woman's wit is on that account all the more diligently to be cultivated, that nature's defect may be redressed by industry. This was the opinion of the ancients, of those who were most prudent as well as most holy. Not to speak of the rest, St. Jerome and St. Augustine not only exhorted excellent matrons and most noble virgins to study, but also, in order to assist them, diligently explained the abstruse meanings of Holy Scripture, and wrote for tender girls letters replete with so much erudition, that nowadays old men, who call themselves professors of sacred science, can scarcely read them correctly, much less understand them. Do you, my learned Gunnell, have the kindness to see that my daughters thoroughly learn these works of those holy men? From them they will learn in particular what end they should propose to themselves in their studies and what is the fruit of their endeavours, namely the testimony of God and a good conscience. Thus peace and calm will abide in their hearts and they will be disturbed neither by fulsome flattery nor by the stupidity of those illiterate men who despise learning.

I fancy that I hear you object that these precepts, though true, are beyond the capacity of my young children, since you will scarcely find a man, however old and advanced, whose mind is so firmly set as not to be tickled sometimes with desire of glory. But, dear Gunnell, the more I see the difficulty of getting rid of this pest of pride, the more do I see the necessity of getting to work at it from childhood. For I find no other reason why this evil clings so to our hearts, than because almost as soon as we are born, it is sown in the tender minds of children by their nurses, it is cultivated by their teachers, and brought to its full growth by their parents; no one teaching even what is good without, at the same time, awakening the expectation of praise, as of the proper reward of virtue. Thus we grow accustomed to make so much of praise, that while we study how to please the greater number (who will always be the worst) we grow ashamed of being good (with the few). That this plague of vainglory may be banished far from my children, I do desire that you, my dear Gunnell, and their mother and all their friends, would sing this song to them, and repeat it, and beat it into their heads, that vainglory is a thing despicable, and to be spit upon; and that there is nothing more sublime than that humble modesty so often praised by Christ; and this your prudent charity will so enforce as to teach virtue rather than reprove vice, and make them love good advice instead of hating it. To this purpose nothing will more conduce than to read to them the lessons of the ancient Fathers, who, they know, cannot be angry with them; and, as they honor them for their sanctity, they must needs be much moved by their authority. If you will teach something of this sort, in addition to their lesson in Sallust—to Margaret and Elizabeth, as being more advanced than John and Cecily—you will bind me and them still more to you. And thus you will bring about that my children, who are dear to me by nature, and still more dear by learning and virtue, will become most dear by that advance in knowledge and good conduct. Adieu.

FROM THE COURT ON THE VIGIL OF PENTECOST.

Thomas More

notes

notes

The Rule of St. Benedict

ST. BENEDICT

CHAPTER 7: OF HUMILITY

BRETHREN, the Holy Scripture crieth to us saying: "Every one that exalteth himself shall be humbled; and he that humbleth himself shall be exalted" (Lk. 14:11; 18:14). Since, therefore, it saith this, it showeth us that every exaltation is a kind of pride. The Prophet declareth that he guardeth himself against this, saying: "Lord, my heart is not puffed up; nor are my eyes haughty. Neither have I walked in great matters nor in wonderful things above me" (Ps. 130[131]:1). What then? "If I was not humbly minded, but exalted my soul; as a child that is weaned is towards his mother so shalt Thou reward my soul" (Ps. 130[131]:2). Hence, brethren, if we wish to reach the greatest height of humility, and speedily to arrive at that heavenly exaltation to which ascent is made in the present life by humility, then, mounting by our actions, we must erect the ladder which appeared to Jacob in his dream, by means of which angels were shown to him ascending and descending (cf. Gen. 28:12).

Without a doubt, we understand this ascending and descending to be nothing else but that we descend by pride and ascend by humility. The erected ladder, however, is our life in the present world, which, if the heart is humble, is by the Lord lifted up to heaven. For we say that our body and our soul are the two sides of this ladder; and into these sides the divine calling hath inserted various degrees of humility or discipline which we must mount. The first degree of humility, then, is that a man always have the fear of God before his eyes (cf. Ps. 35[36]:2), shunning all forgetfulness and that he be ever mindful of all that God hath commanded, that he always considereth in his mind how those who despise God will burn in hell for their sins, and that life everlasting is prepared for those who fear God. And whilst he guardeth himself evermore against sin and vices of thought, word, deed, and self-will, let him also hasten to cut off the desires of the flesh.

Let a man consider that God always seeth him from Heaven, that the eye of God beholdeth his works everywhere, and that the angels report them to Him every hour. The Prophet telleth us this when he showeth God thus ever present in our thoughts, saying: "The searcher of hearts and reins is God" (Ps. 7:10). And again: "The Lord knoweth the thoughts of men" (Ps. 93[94]:11) And he saith: "Thou hast understood my thoughts afar off" (Ps. 138[139]:3). And: "The thoughts of man shall give praise to Thee" (Ps. 75[76]:11). Therefore, in order that he may always be on his guard against evil thoughts, let the humble brother always say in his heart: "Then I shall be spotless before Him, if I shall keep myself from iniquity" (Ps. 17[18]:24).

We are thus forbidden to do our own will, since the Scripture saith to us: "And turn away from thy evil will" (Sir. 18:30). And thus, too, we ask God in prayer that His will may be done in us (cf. Mt. 6:10). We are, therefore, rightly taught not to do our own will, when we guard against what Scripture saith: "There are ways that to men seem right, the end whereof plungeth into the depths of hell" (Prov. 16:25). And also when we are filled with dread at what is said of the negligent: "They are corrupted and become abominable in their pleasure" (Ps. 13[14]:1). But as regards desires of the flesh, let us believe that God is thus ever present to us, since the Prophet saith to the Lord: "Before Thee is all my desire" (Ps. 37[38]:10).

We must, therefore, guard thus against evil desires, because death hath his station near the entrance of pleasure. Whence the Scripture commandeth, saying: "Go no after thy lusts" (Sir. 18:30). If, therefore, the eyes of the Lord observe the good and the bad (cf. Prov. 15:3) and the Lord always looketh down from heaven on the children of men, to see whether there be anyone that understandeth or seeketh God (cf. Ps. 13[14]:2); and if our actions are reported to the Lord day and night by the angels who are appointed to watch over us daily, we must ever be on our guard, brethren, as the Prophet saith in the psalm, that God may at no time see us "gone aside to evil and become unprofitable" (Ps. 13[14]:3), and having spared us in the present time, because He is kind and waiteth for us to be changed for the better, say to us in the future: "These things thou hast done and I was silent" (Ps. 49[50]:21). The second degree of humility is, when a man loveth not his own will, nor is pleased to fulfill his own desires but by his deeds carrieth out that word of the Lord which saith: "I came not to do my own will but the will of Him that sent me" (Jn, 6:38). It is likewise said: "Self-will hath its punishment, but necessity winneth the crown." The third degree of humility is, that for the love of God a man subject himself to a Superior in all obedience, imitating the Lord, of whom the Apostle saith: "He became obedient unto death" (Phil. 2:8). The fourth degree of humility is, that, if hard and distasteful things are commanded, nay, even though injuries are inflicted, he accept them with patience and even temper, and not grow weary or give up, but hold out, as the Scripture saith: "He that shall persevere unto the end shall be saved" (Mt. 10:22). And again: "Let thy heart take courage, and wait thou for the Lord" (Ps. 26[27]:14). And showing that a faithful man ought even to bear every disagreeable thing for the Lord, it saith in the person of the suffering: "For Thy sake we suffer death all the day long; we are counted as sheep for the slaughter" (Rom. 8:36; Ps. 43[44]:22).

And secure in the hope of the divine reward, they go on

joyfully, saying: "But in all these things we overcome because of Him that hath loved us" (Rom. 8:37). And likewise in another place the Scripture saith: "Thou, O God, hast proved us; Thou hast tried us by fire as silver is tried; Thou hast brought us into a net; Thou hast laid afflictions on our back" (Ps. 65[66]:10–11). And to show us that we ought to be under a Superior, it continueth, saying: "Thou hast set men over our heads" (Ps. 65[66]:12). And fulfilling the command of the Lord by patience also in adversities and injuries, when struck on the one cheek they turn also the other; the despoiler of their coat they give their cloak also; and when forced to go one mile they go two (cf. Mt. 5:39–41); with the Apostle Paul they bear with false brethren and "bless those who curse them" (2 Cor. 11:26; 1 Cor. 4:12).

The fifth degree of humility is, when one hideth from his Abbot none of the evil thoughts which rise in his heart or the evils committed by him in secret, but humbly confesseth them. Concerning this the Scripture exhorts us, saying: "Reveal thy way to the Lord and trust in Him" (Ps. 36[37]:5). And it saith further: "Confess to the Lord, for He is good, for His mercy endureth forever" (Ps. 105[106]:1; Ps. 117[118]:1). And the Prophet likewise saith: "I have acknowledged my sin to Thee and my injustice I have not concealed. I said I will confess against myself my injustice to the Lord; and Thou hast forgiven the wickedness of my sins" (Ps. 31[32]:5).

The sixth degree of humility is, when a monk is content with the meanest and worst of everything, and in all that is

enjoined him holdeth himself as a bad and worthless work-
man, saying with the Prophet: "I am brought to nothing and
I knew it not; I am become as a beast before Thee, and I am
always with Thee" (Ps. 72[73]:22–23). The seventh degree of
humility is, when, not only with his tongue he declareth, but
also in his inmost soul believeth, that he is the lowest and
vilest of men, humbling himself and saying with the Prophet:
"But I am a worm and no man, the reproach of men and the
outcast of the people" (Ps. 21[22]:7). "I have been exalted
and humbled and confounded" (Ps. 87[88]:16). And also: "It
is good for me that Thou hast humbled me, that I may learn
Thy commandments" (Ps. 118[119]:71,73).

The eighth degree of humility is, when a monk doeth
nothing but what is sanctioned by the common rule of the
monastery and the example of his elders. The ninth degree
of humility is, when a monk withholdeth his tongue from
speaking, and keeping silence doth not speak until he is
asked; for the Scripture showeth that "in a multitude of words
there shall not want sin" (Prov. 10:19); and that "a man full of
tongue is not established in the earth" (Ps. 139[140]:12). The
tenth degree of humility is, when a monk is not easily moved
and quick for laughter, for it is written: "The fool exalteth his
voice in laughter" (Sir. 21:23).

The eleventh degree of humility is, that, when a monk
speaketh, he speak gently and without laughter, humbly and
with gravity, with few and sensible words, and that he be
not loud of voice, as it is written: "The wise man is known

by the fewness of his words." The twelfth degree of humility is, when a monk is not only humble of heart, but always letteth it appear also in his whole exterior to all that see him; namely, at the Work of God, in the garden, on a journey, in the field, or wherever he may be, sitting, walking, or standing, let him always have his head bowed down, his eyes fixed on the ground, ever holding himself guilty of his sins, thinking that he is already standing before the dread judgment seat of God, and always saying to himself in his heart what the publican in the Gospel said, with his eyes fixed on the ground: "Lord, I am a sinner and not worthy to lift up mine eyes to heaven" (Lk. 18:13); and again with the Prophet: "I am bowed down and humbled exceedingly" (Ps. 37[38]:7–9; Ps. 118[119]:107).

Having, therefore, ascended all these degrees of humility, the monk will presently arrive at that love of God, which being perfect, casteth out fear (1 Jn. 4:18). In virtue of this love all things which at first he observed not without fear, he will now begin to keep without any effort, and as it were, naturally by force of habit, no longer from the fear of hell, but from the love of Christ, from the very habit of good and the pleasure in virtue. May the Lord be pleased to manifest all this by His Holy Spirit in His laborer now cleansed from vice and sin.

notes

The Rule

notes

PART II
Liberty and the City

Federalist 51

JAMES MADISON

TO THE PEOPLE OF THE STATE OF NEW YORK

To what expedient, then, shall we finally resort, for maintaining in practice the necessary partition of power among the several departments, as laid down in the Constitution? The only answer that can be given is, that as all these exterior provisions are found to be inadequate, the defect must be supplied, by so contriving the interior structure of the government as that its several constituent parts may, by their mutual relations, be the means of keeping each other in their proper places. Without presuming to undertake a full development of this important idea, I will hazard a few general observations, which may perhaps place it in a clearer light, and enable us to form a more correct judgment of the principles and structure of the government planned by the convention.

In order to lay a due foundation for that separate and distinct exercise of the different powers of government, which to a certain extent is admitted on all hands to be essential to the preservation of liberty, it is evident that each department should have a will of its own; and consequently should be so constituted that the members of each should have as little agency as possible in the appointment of the members of the others. Were this principle rigorously adhered to, it would require that all the appointments for the supreme executive, legislative, and judiciary magistracies should be drawn from the same fountain of authority, the people, through channels having no communication whatever with one another. Perhaps such a plan of constructing the several departments would be less difficult in practice than it may in contemplation appear. Some difficulties, however, and some additional expense would attend the execution of it. Some deviations, therefore, from the principle must be admitted. In the constitution of the judiciary department in particular, it might be inexpedient to insist rigorously on the principle: first, because peculiar qualifications being essential in the members, the primary consideration ought to be to select that mode of choice which best secures these qualifications; secondly, because the permanent tenure by which the appointments are held in that department, must soon destroy all sense of dependence on the authority conferring them.

It is equally evident, that the members of each department should be as little dependent as possible on those of the others, for the emoluments annexed to their offices. Were the executive magistrate, or the judges, not independent of the legislature in this particular, their independence in every other would be merely nominal. But the great security against a gradual concentration of the several powers in the same department, consists in giving to those who administer each department the necessary constitutional means and personal motives to resist encroachments of the others. The provision for defense must in this, as in all other cases, be made commensurate to the danger of attack. Ambition must be made to counteract ambition. The interest of the man must be connected with the constitutional rights of the place. It may be a reflection on human nature, that such devices should be necessary to control the abuses of government. But what is government itself, but the greatest of all reflections on human nature? If men were angels, no government would be necessary. If angels were to govern men, neither external nor internal controls on government would be necessary. In framing a government which is to be administered by men over men, the great difficulty lies in this: you must first enable the government to control the governed; and in the next place oblige it to control itself....

In a free government the security for civil rights must be the same as that for religious rights. It consists in the one case in the multiplicity of interests, and in the other in the multiplicity of sects. The degree of security in both cases will depend on the number of interests and sects; and this may be presumed to depend on the extent of country and number of people comprehended under the same government. This view of the subject must particularly recommend a proper federal system to all the sincere and considerate friends of republican government, since it shows that in exact proportion as the territory of the Union may be formed into more circumscribed Confederacies, or States oppressive combinations of a majority will be facilitated: the best security, under the republican forms, for the rights of every class of citizens, will be diminished: and consequently the stability and independence of some member of the government, the only other security, must be proportionately increased. Justice is the end of government. It is the end of civil society. It ever has been and ever will be pursued until it be obtained, or until liberty be lost in the pursuit. In a society under the forms of which the stronger faction can readily unite and oppress the weaker, anarchy may as truly be said to reign as in a state of nature, where the weaker individual is not secured against the violence of the stronger; and as, in the latter state, even the stronger individuals are prompted, by the uncertainty of their condition, to submit to a government which may protect the weak as well as themselves; so, in the former state, will the more powerful factions or parties be gradually induced, by a like motive, to wish for a government which will protect all parties, the weaker as well as the more powerful.

It can be little doubted that if the State of Rhode Island was separated from the Confederacy and left to itself, the insecurity of rights under the popular form of government within such narrow limits would be displayed by such reiterated oppressions of factious majorities that some power altogether independent of the people would soon be called for by the voice of the very factions whose misrule had proved the necessity of it. In the extended republic of the United States, and among the great variety of interests, parties, and sects which it embraces, a coalition of a majority of the whole society could seldom take place on any other principles than those of justice and the general good; whilst there being thus less danger to a minor from the will of a major party, there must be less pretext, also, to provide for the security of the former, by introducing into the government a will not dependent on the latter, or, in other words, a will independent of the society itself. It is no less certain than it is important, notwithstanding the contrary opinions which have been entertained, that the larger the society, provided it lie within a practical sphere, the more duly capable it will be of self-government. And happily for the REPUBLICAN CAUSE, the practicable sphere may be carried to a very great extent, by a judicious modification and mixture of the FEDERAL PRINCIPLE.

Publius

THE BLESSINGS OF LIBERTY

notes

notes

Summa Theologiae I-II, q. 105, a. 1

ST. THOMAS AQUINAS

QUESTION 105, ARTICLE 1: *Whether the Old Law enjoined fitting precepts concerning rulers?*

OBJECTION 1. It would seem that the Old Law made unfitting precepts concerning rulers. Because, as the Philosopher says (*Polit.* III, 4), "the ordering of the people depends mostly on the chief ruler." But the Law contains no precept relating to the institution of the chief ruler; and yet we find therein prescriptions concerning the inferior rulers: firstly (Ex. 18:21): "Provide out of all the people wise men," etc.; again (Num. 11:16): "Gather unto me seventy men of the ancients of Israel"; and again (Deut. 1:13): "Let me have from among you wise and understanding men," etc. Therefore the Law provided insufficiently in regard to the rulers of the people.

OBJECTION 2. Further, "The best gives of the best," as Plato states (*Tim.* II). Now the best ordering of a state or of any nation is to be ruled by a king: because this kind of government approaches nearest in resemblance to the Divine government, whereby God rules the world from the beginning. Therefore the Law should have set a king over the people, and they should not have been allowed a choice in the matter, as indeed they were allowed (Deut. 17:14–15): "When thou... shalt say: I will set a king over me...thou shalt set him," etc.

OBJECTION 3. Further, according to Matthew 12:25: "Every kingdom divided against itself shall be made desolate": a saying which was verified in the Jewish people, whose destruction was brought about by the division of the kingdom. But the Law should aim chiefly at things pertaining to the general well-being of the people. Therefore it should have forbidden the kingdom to be divided under two kings: nor should this have been introduced even by Divine authority; as we read of its being introduced by the authority of the prophet Ahias the Silonite (1 Kgs. 11:29ff.).

OBJECTION 4. Further, just as priests are instituted for the benefit of the people in things concerning God, as stated in Hebrews 5:1; so are rulers set up for the benefit of the people in human affairs. But certain things were allotted as a means of livelihood for the priests and Levites of the Law: such as the tithes and first-fruits, and many like things. Therefore in like manner certain things should have been determined for the livelihood of the rulers of the people: the more that they were forbidden to accept presents, as is clearly stated in Exodus 23:8: "You shall not take bribes, which even blind the wise, and pervert the words of the just."

OBJECTION 5. Further, as a kingdom is the best form of government, so is tyranny the most corrupt. But when the Lord appointed the king, He established a tyrannical law; for it is written (1 Sam. 8:11): "This will be the right of the king, that shall reign over you: He will take your sons," etc. Therefore the Law made unfitting provision with regard to the institution of rulers.

ON THE CONTRARY, The people of Israel is commended for the beauty of its order (Num. 24:5): "How beautiful are thy tabernacles, O Jacob, and thy tents." But the beautiful ordering of a people depends on the right establishment of its rulers. Therefore the Law made right provision for the people with regard to its rulers.

I ANSWER THAT, Two points are to be observed concerning the right ordering of rulers in a state or nation. One is that all should take some share in the government: for this form of constitution ensures peace among the people, commends itself to all, and is most enduring, as stated in *Polit.* II, 6. The other point is to be observed in respect of the kinds of government, or the different ways in which the constitutions are established. For whereas these differ in kind, as the Philosopher states (*Polit.* III, 5), nevertheless the first place is held by the "kingdom," where the power of government is vested in one; and "aristocracy," which signifies government by the best, where the power of government is vested in a few. Accordingly, the best form of government is in a state or kingdom, where one is given the power to preside over all; while under him are others having governing powers: and yet a government of this kind is shared by all, both because all are eligible to govern, and because the rules are chosen by all. For this is the best form of polity, being partly kingdom, since there is one at the head of all; partly aristocracy, in so far as a number of persons are set in authority; partly democracy, i.e., government by the people, in so far as the rulers can be chosen from the people, and the people have the right to choose their rulers.

Such was the form of government established by the Divine Law. For Moses and his successors governed the people in such a way that each of them was ruler over all; so that there was a kind of kingdom. Moreover, seventy-two men were chosen, who were elders in virtue: for it is written (Deut. 1:15): "I took out of your tribes wise and honorable, and appointed them rulers": so that there was an element of aristocracy. But it was a democratical government in so far as the rulers were chosen from all the people; for it is written (Ex. 18:21): "Provide out of all the people wise men," etc.;

and, again, in so far as they were chosen by the people; where-fore it is written (Deut. 1:13): "Let me have from among you wise men," etc. Consequently it is evident that the ordering of the rulers was well provided for by the Law.

REPLY TO OBJECTION 1. This people was governed under the special care of God: wherefore it is written (Deut. 7:6): "The Lord thy God hath chosen thee to be His peculiar people": and this is why the Lord reserved to Himself the institution of the chief ruler. For this too did Moses pray (Num. 27:16): "May the Lord the God of the spirits of all the flesh pro-vide a man, that may be over this multitude." Thus by God's orders Joshua was set at the head in place of Moses; and we read about each of the judges who succeeded Josue that God "raised...up a savior" for the people, and that "the spirit of the Lord was" in them (Judg. 3:9–15). Hence the Lord did not leave the choice of a king to the people; but reserved this to Himself, as appears from Deuteronomy 17:15: "Thou shalt set him whom the Lord thy God shall choose."

REPLY TO OBJECTION 2. A kingdom is the best form of gov-ernment of the people, so long as it is not corrupt. But since the power granted to a king is so great, it easily degenerates into tyranny, unless he to whom this power is given be a very virtuous man: for it is only the virtuous man that conducts himself well in the midst of prosperity, as the Philosopher observes (*Ethic.* IV, 3). Now perfect virtue is to be found in few: and especially were the Jews inclined to cruelty and avarice, which vices above all turn men into tyrants. Hence from the very first the Lord did not set up the kingly authority with full power, but gave them judges and governors to rule them. But afterwards when the people asked Him to do so, being indignant with them, so to speak, He granted them a king, as is clear from His words to Samuel (1 Sam. 8:7): "They have not rejected thee, but me, that I should not reign over them."

Nevertheless, as regards the appointment of a king, He did establish the manner of election from the very beginning (Deut. 17:14ff.): and then He determined two points: first, that in choosing a king they should wait for the Lord's decision; and that they should not make a man of another nation king, because such kings are wont to take little interest in the people they are set over, and consequently to have no care for their welfare: secondly, He prescribed how the king after his appointment should behave, in regard to himself; namely, that he should not accumulate chariots and horses, nor wives, nor immense wealth: because through craving for such things princes become tyrants and forsake justice. He also appointed the manner in which they were to conduct themselves towards God: namely, that they should continually read and ponder on God's Law, and should ever fear and obey God. Moreover, He decided how they should behave towards their subjects: namely, that they should not proudly despise them, or ill-treat them, and that they should not depart from the paths of justice.

REPLY TO OBJECTION 3. The division of the kingdom, and a number of kings, was rather a punishment inflicted on that people for their many dissensions, specially against the just rule of David, than a benefit conferred on them for their profit. Hence it is written (Hos. 13:11): "I will give thee a king in my wrath"; and (Hos. 8:4): "They have reigned, but not by me: they have been princes, and I knew not."

REPLY TO OBJECTION 4. The priestly office was bequeathed by succession from father to son: and this, in order that it might be held in greater respect, if not any man from the people could become a priest: since honor was given to them out of reverence for the divine worship. Hence it was necessary to put aside certain things for them both as to tithes and as to first-fruits, and, again, as to oblations and sacrifices, that they might be afforded a means of livelihood. On the other hand, the rulers, as stated above, were chosen from the whole people; wherefore they had their own possessions, from which to derive a living: and so much the more, since the Lord forbade even a king to have superabundant wealth to make too much show of magnificence: both because he could scarcely avoid the excesses of pride and tyranny, arising from such things, and because, if the rulers were not very rich, and if their office involved much work and anxiety, it would not tempt the ambition of the common people; and would not become an occasion of sedition.

REPLY TO OBJECTION 5. That right was not given to the king by Divine institution; rather was it foretold that kings would usurp that right, by framing unjust laws, and by degenerating into tyrants who preyed on their subjects. This is clear from the context that follows: "And you shall be his slaves": which is significative of tyranny, since a tyrant rules is subjects as though they were his slaves. Hence Samuel spoke these words to deter them from asking for a king; since the narrative continues: "But the people would not hear the voice of Samuel." It may happen, however, that even a good king, without being a tyrant, may take away the sons, and make them tribunes and centurions; and may take many things from his subjects in order to secure the common weal.

notes

THE BLESSINGS OF LIBERTY

notes

My Kinsman, Major Molineux

NATHANIEL HAWTHORNE

After the kings of Great Britain had assumed the right of appointing the colonial governors, the measures of the latter seldom met with the ready and general approbation which had been paid to those of their predecessors, under the original charters. The people looked with most jealous scrutiny to the exercise of power which did not emanate from themselves, and they usually rewarded their rulers with slender gratitude for the compliances by which, in softening their instructions from beyond the sea, they had incurred the reprehension of those who gave them. The annals of Massachusetts Bay will inform us, that of six governors in the space of about forty years from the surrender of the old charter, under James II, two were imprisoned by a popular insurrection; a third, as Hutchinson inclines to believe, was driven from the province by the whizzing of a musket-ball; a fourth, in the opinion of the same historian, was hastened to his grave by continual bickerings with the House of Representatives; and the remaining two, as well as their successors, till the Revolution, were favored with few and brief intervals of peaceful sway. The inferior members of the court party, in times of high political excitement, led scarcely a more desirable life. These remarks may serve as a preface to the following adventures, which chanced upon a summer night, not far from a hundred years ago. The reader, in order to avoid a long and dry detail of colonial affairs, is requested to dispense with an account of the train of circumstances that had caused much temporary inflammation of the popular mind.

It was near nine o'clock of a moonlight evening, when a boat crossed the ferry with a single passenger, who had obtained his conveyance at that unusual hour by the promise of an extra fare. While he stood on the landing-place, searching in either pocket for the means of fulfilling his agreement, the ferryman lifted a lantern, by the aid of which, and the newly risen moon, he took a very accurate survey of the stranger's figure. He was a youth of barely eighteen years, evidently country-bred, and now, as it should seem, upon his first visit to town. He was clad in a coarse grey coat, well worn, but in excellent repair; his under garments were durably constructed of leather, and fitted tight to a pair of serviceable and well-shaped limbs; his stockings of blue yarn were the incontrovertible work of a mother or a sister; and on his head was a three-cornered hat, which in its better days had perhaps sheltered the graver brow of the lad's father. Under his left arm was a heavy cudgel, formed of an oak sapling, and retaining a part of the hardened root; and his equipment was completed by a wallet, not so abundantly stocked as to incommode the vigorous shoulders on which it hung. Brown, curly hair, well-shaped features, and bright, cheerful eyes were nature's gifts, and worth all that art could have done for his adornment.

The youth, one of whose names was Robin, finally drew from his pocket the half of a little province bill of five shillings, which, in the depreciation of that sort of currency, did but satisfy the ferryman's demand, with the surplus of a sexangular piece of parchment, valued at three pence. He then walked forward into the town, with as light a step as if his day's journey had not already exceeded thirty miles, and with as eager an eye as if he were entering London city, instead of the little metropolis of a New England colony. Before Robin had proceeded far, however, it occurred to him that he knew not whither to direct his steps; so he paused, and looked up and down the narrow street, scrutinizing the small and mean wooden buildings that were scattered on either side.

"This low hovel cannot be my kinsman's dwelling," thought he, "nor yonder old house, where the moonlight enters at the broken casement; and truly I see none hereabouts that might be worthy of him. It would have been wise to enquire my way of the ferryman, and doubtless he would have gone with me, and earned a shilling from the Major for his pains. But the next man I meet will do as well."

He resumed his walk, and was glad to perceive that the street now became wider, and the houses more respectable in their appearance. He soon discerned a figure moving on moderately in advance, and hastened his steps to overtake it. As Robin drew nigh, he saw that the passenger was a man in years, with a full periwig of grey hair, a wide-skirted coat of dark cloth, and silk stockings rolled above his knees. He carried a long and polished cane, which he struck down perpendicularly before him, at every step; and at regular intervals he uttered two successive hems, of a peculiarly solemn and sepulchral intonation. Having made these observations, Robin laid hold of the skirt of the old man's coat, just when the light from the open door and windows of a barber's shop fell upon both their figures.

"Good evening to you, honored sir," said he, making a low bow, and still retaining his hold of the skirt. "I pray you tell me whereabouts is the dwelling of my kinsman, Major Molineux."

The youth's question was uttered very loudly; and one of the barbers, whose razor was descending on a well-soaped chin, and another who was dressing a Ramillies wig, left their occupations, and came to the door. The citizen, in the meantime, turned a long-favored countenance upon Robin, and answered him in a tone of excessive anger and annoyance. His two sepulchral hems, however, broke into the very center of his rebuke, with most singular effect, like a thought of the cold grave obtruding among wrathful passions.

"Let go my garment, fellow! I tell you, I know not the man you speak of. What! I have authority, I have—hem, hem—authority; and if this be the respect you show for your betters, your feet shall be brought acquainted with the stocks by daylight, tomorrow morning!"

Robin released the old man's skirt, and hastened away, pursued by an ill-mannered roar of laughter from the barber's shop. He was at first considerably surprised by the result of his question, but, being a shrewd youth, soon thought himself able to account for the mystery.

"This is some country representative," was his conclusion, "who has never seen the inside of my kinsman's door, and lacks the breeding to answer a stranger civilly. The man is old, or verily—I might be tempted to turn back and smite him on the nose. Ah, Robin, Robin! Even the barber's boys laugh at you for choosing such a guide! You will be wiser in time, friend Robin."

He now became entangled in a succession of crooked and narrow streets, which crossed each other, and meandered at no great distance from the waterside. The smell of tar was obvious to his nostrils, the masts of vessels pierced the moonlight above the tops of the buildings, and the numerous signs, which Robin paused to read, informed him that he was near the center of business. But the streets were empty, the shops were closed, and lights were visible only in the second stories of a few dwelling-houses. At length, on the corner of a narrow lane, through which he was passing, he beheld the broad countenance of a British hero swinging before the door of an inn, whence proceeded the voices of many guests. The casement of one of the lower windows was thrown back, and a very thin curtain permitted Robin to distinguish a party at supper, round a well-furnished table. The fragrance of the good cheer steamed forth into the outer air, and the youth could not fail to recollect that the last remnant of his travelling stock of provision had yielded to his morning appetite, and that noon had found and left him dinnerless.

"O, that a parchment three-penny might give me a right to sit at yonder table!" said Robin, with a sigh. "But the Major will make me welcome to the best of his victuals; so I will even step boldly in, and inquire my way to his dwelling."

He entered the tavern, and was guided by the murmur of voices and the fumes of tobacco to the public room. It was a long and low apartment, with oaken walls, grown dark in the continual smoke, and a floor which was thickly sanded, but of no immaculate purity. A number of persons—the larger part of whom appeared to be mariners, or in some way connected with the sea—occupied the wooden benches, or leather-bottomed chairs, conversing on various matters, and occasionally lending their attention to some topic of general interest. Three or four little groups were draining as many bowls of punch, which the West India trade had long since made a familiar drink in the colony. Others, who had the appearance of men who lived by regular and laborious handicraft, preferred the insulated bliss of an unshared potation, and became more taciturn under its influence. Nearly all, in short, evinced a predilection for the Good Creature in some of its various shapes, for this is a vice to which, as Fast-day sermons of a hundred years ago will testify, we have a long hereditary claim. The only guests to whom Robin's sympathies inclined him were two or three sheepish countrymen, who were using the inn somewhat after the fashion of a Turkish caravansary; they had gotten themselves into the darkest corner of the room, and, heedless of the Nicotian atmosphere, were supping on the bread of their own ovens, and the bacon cured in their own chimney-smoke. But though Robin felt a sort of brotherhood with these strangers, his eyes were attracted from them to a person who stood near the door, holding whispered conversation with a group of ill-dressed associates. His features were separately striking almost to grotesqueness, and the whole face left a deep impression on the memory. The forehead bulged out into a double prominence, with a vale between; the nose came boldly forth in an irregular curve, and its bridge was of more than a finger's breadth; the eyebrows were deep and shaggy, and the eyes glowed beneath them like fire in a cave.

While Robin deliberated of whom to inquire respecting his kinsman's dwelling, he was accosted by the innkeeper, a little man in a stained white apron, who had come to pay his professional welcome to the stranger. Being in the second generation from a French Protestant, he seemed to have inherited the courtesy of his parent nation; but no variety of circumstances was ever known to change his voice from the one shrill note in which he now addressed Robin.

"From the country, I presume, sir?" said he, with a profound bow. "Beg leave to congratulate you on your arrival, and trust you intend a long stay with us. Fine town here, sir, beautiful buildings, and much that may interest a stranger. May I hope for the honor of your commands in respect to supper?"

"The man sees a family likeness! The rogue has guessed that I am related to the Major!" thought Robin, who had hitherto experienced little superfluous civility.

All eyes were now turned on the country lad, standing at the door, in his worn three-cornered hat, grey coat, leather breeches, and blue yarn stockings, leaning on an oaken cudgel, and bearing a wallet on his back.

Robin replied to the courteous innkeeper, with such an assumption of confidence as befitted the Major's relative. "My honest friend," he said, "I shall make it a point to patronize your house on some occasion, when"—here he could not help lowering his voice—"when I may have more than a parchment threepence in my pocket. My present business," continued he, speaking with lofty confidence, "is merely to inquire my way to the dwelling of my kinsman, Major Molineux."

There was a sudden and general movement in the room, which Robin interpreted as expressing the eagerness of each individual to become his guide. But the innkeeper turned his eyes to a written paper on the wall, which he read, or seemed to read, with occasional recurrences to the young man's figure. "What have we here?" said he, breaking his speech into little dry fragments. "'Left the house of the subscriber, bounden servant, Hezekiah Mudge—had on, when he went away, grey coat, leather breeches, master's third-best hat. One pound currency reward to whosoever shall lodge him in any jail of the province.' Better trudge, boy, better trudge!"

Robin had begun to draw his hand towards the lighter end of the oak cudgel, but a strange hostility in every countenance induced him to relinquish his purpose of breaking the courteous innkeeper's head. As he turned to leave the room, he encountered a sneering glance from the bold-featured personage whom he had before noticed; and no sooner was he beyond the door, than he heard a general laugh, in which the innkeeper's voice might be distinguished, like the dropping of small stones into a kettle.

"Now, is it not strange," thought Robin, with his usual shrewdness, "is it not strange that the confession of an empty pocket should outweigh the name of my kinsman, Major Molineux? Oh, if I had one of those grinning rascals in the woods, where I and my oak sapling grew up together, I would teach him that my arm is heavy, though my purse be light!"

On turning the corner of the narrow lane, Robin found himself in a spacious street, with an unbroken line of lofty houses on each side, and a steepled building at the upper end, whence the ringing of a bell announced the hour of nine. The light of the moon, and the lamps from the numerous shop-windows, discovered people promenading on the pavement, and amongst them Robin hoped to recognize his hitherto inscrutable relative. The result of his former inquiries made him unwilling to hazard another, in a scene of such publicity, and he determined to walk slowly and silently up the street, thrusting his face close to that of every elderly gentleman, in search of the Major's lineaments. In his progress, Robin encountered many gay and gallant figures. Embroidered garments of showy colors, enormous periwigs, gold-laced hats, and silver-hilted swords glided past him and dazzled his optics. Travelled youths, imitators of the European fine gentlemen of the period, trod jauntily along, half-dancing to the fashionable tunes which they hummed, and making poor Robin ashamed of his quiet and natural gait. At length, after many pauses to examine the gorgeous display of goods in the shop-windows, and after suffering some rebukes for the impertinence of his scrutiny into people's faces, the Major's kinsman found himself near the steepled building, still unsuccessful in his search. As yet, however he had seen only one side of the thronged street, so Robin crossed, and continued the same sort of inquisition down the opposite pavement, with stronger hopes than the philosopher seeking an honest man, but with no better fortune. He had arrived about midway towards the lower end, from which his course began, when he overheard the approach of someone who struck down a cane on the flagstones at every step, uttering, at regular intervals, two sepulchral hems.

"Mercy on us!" quoth Robin, recognizing the sound.

Turning a corner, which chanced to be close at his right hand, he hastened to pursue his researches in some other part of the town. His patience now was wearing low, and he seemed to feel more fatigue from his rambles since he crossed the ferry, than from his journey of several days on the other side. Hunger also pleaded loudly within him, and Robin began to balance the propriety of demanding violently, and with lifted cudgel, the necessary guidance from the first solitary passenger whom he should meet. While a resolution to this effect was gaining strength, he entered a street of mean appearance, on either side of which a row of ill-built houses was straggling towards the harbor. The moonlight fell upon no passenger along the whole extent, but in the third domicile which Robin passed there was a half-opened door, and his keen glance detected a woman's garment within.

"My luck may be better here," said he to himself.

Accordingly, he approached the door, and beheld it shut closer as he did so; yet an open space remained, sufficing for the fair occupant to observe the stranger, without a corresponding display on her part. All that Robin could discern was a strip of scarlet petticoat, and the occasional sparkle of an eye, as if the moonbeams were trembling on some bright thing.

"Pretty mistress"—for I may call her so with a good conscience, thought the shrewd youth, since I know nothing to the contrary—"my sweet pretty mistress, will you be kind enough to tell me whereabouts I must seek the dwelling of my kinsman, Major Molineux?"

Robin's voice was plaintive and winning, and the female, seeing nothing to be shunned in the handsome country youth, thrust open the door, and came forth into the moonlight. She was a dainty little figure, with a white neck, round arms, and a slender waist, at the extremity of which her scarlet petticoat jutted out over a hoop, as if she were standing in a balloon. Moreover, her face was oval and pretty, her hair dark beneath the little cap, and her bright eyes possessed a sly freedom, which triumphed over those of Robin.

"Major Molineux dwells here," said this fair woman.

Now, her voice was the sweetest Robin had heard that night, the airy counterpart of a stream of melted silver; yet he could not help doubting whether that sweet voice spoke Gospel truth. He looked up and down the mean street, and then surveyed the house before which they stood. It was a small, dark edifice of two stories, the second of which projected over the lower floor; and the front apartment had the aspect of a shop for petty commodities.

"Now, truly, I am in luck," replied Robin, cunningly, "and so indeed is my kinsman, the Major, in having so pretty a housekeeper. But I prithee trouble him to step to the door; I will deliver him a message from his friends in the country, and then go back to my lodgings at the inn."

"Nay, the Major has been abed this hour or more," said the lady of the scarlet petticoat; "and it would be to little purpose to disturb him tonight, seeing his evening draught was of the strongest. But he is a kind-hearted man, and it would be as much as my life's worth to let a kinsman of his turn away from the door. You are the good old gentleman's very picture, and I could swear that was his rainy-weather hat. Also he has garments very much resembling those leather small-clothes. But come in, I pray, for I bid you hearty welcome in his name."

So saying, the fair and hospitable dame took our hero by the hand; and the touch was light, and the force was gentleness, and though Robin read in her eyes what he did not hear in her words, yet the slender-waisted woman in the scarlet petticoat proved stronger than the athletic country youth. She had drawn his half-willing footsteps nearly to the threshold, when the opening of a door in the neighborhood startled the Major's housekeeper, and, leaving the Major's kinsman, she vanished speedily into her own domicile. A heavy yawn preceded the appearance of a man, who, like the Moonshine of Pyramus and Thisbe, carried a lantern, needlessly aiding his sister luminary in the heavens. As he walked sleepily up the street, he turned his broad, dull face on Robin, and displayed a long staff, spiked at the end.

"Home, vagabond, home!" said the watchman, in accents that seemed to fall asleep as soon as they were uttered. "Home, or we'll set you in the stocks, by peep of day!"

"This is the second hint of the kind," thought Robin. "I wish they would end my difficulties, by setting me there tonight."

Nevertheless, the youth felt an instinctive antipathy towards the guardian of midnight order, which at first prevented him from asking his usual question. But just when the man was about to vanish behind the corner, Robin resolved not to lose the opportunity, and shouted lustily after him:

"I say, friend! Will you guide me to the house of my kinsman, Major Molineux?"

The watchman made no reply, but turned the corner and was gone; yet Robin seemed to hear the sound of drowsy laughter stealing along the solitary street. At that moment, also, a pleasant titter saluted him from the open window above his head; he looked up, and caught the sparkle of a saucy eye; a round arm beckoned to him, and next he heard light footsteps descending the staircase within. But Robin, being of the household of a New England clergyman, was a good youth, as well as a shrewd one; so he resisted temptation, and fled away.

He now roamed desperately, and at random, through the town, almost ready to believe that a spell was on him, like that by which a wizard of his country had once kept three pursuers wandering, a whole winter night, within twenty paces of the cottage which they sought. The streets lay before him, strange and desolate, and the lights were extinguished in almost every house. Twice, however, little parties of men, among whom Robin distinguished individuals in outlandish attire, came hurrying along; but though on both occasions they paused to address him, such intercourse did not at all enlighten his perplexity. They did but utter a few words in some language of which Robin knew nothing, and perceiving his inability to answer, bestowed a curse upon him in plain English, and hastened away. Finally, the lad determined to knock at the door of every mansion that might appear worthy to be occupied by his kinsman, trusting that perseverance would overcome the fatality that had hitherto thwarted him. Firm in this resolve, he was passing beneath the walls of a church, which formed the corner of two streets, when, as he turned into the shade of its steeple, he encountered a bulky stranger, muffled in a cloak. The man was proceeding with the speed of earnest business, but Robin planted himself full before him, holding the oak cudgel with both hands across his body as a bar to further passage.

"Halt, honest man, and answer me a question," said he, very resolutely. "Tell me, this instant, whereabouts is the dwelling of my kinsman, Major Molineux!"

"Keep your tongue between your teeth, fool, and let me pass!" said a deep, gruff voice, which Robin partly remembered. "Let me pass, I say, or I'll strike you to the earth!"

"No, no, neighbor!" cried Robin, flourishing his cudgel, and then thrusting its larger end close to the man's muffled face. "No, no, I'm not the fool you take me for, nor do you pass till I have an answer to my question. Whereabouts is the dwelling of my kinsman, Major Molineux?"

The stranger, instead of attempting to force his passage, stepped back into the moonlight, unmuffled his face, and stared full into that of Robin.

"Watch here an hour, and Major Molineux will pass by," said he.

Robin gazed with dismay and astonishment on the unprecedented physiognomy of the speaker. The forehead with its double prominence, the broad hooked nose, the shaggy eyebrows, and fiery eyes were those which he had noticed at the inn, but the man's complexion had undergone a singular, or, more properly, a twofold change. One side of the face blazed an intense red, while the other was black as midnight, the division line being in the broad bridge of the nose: and a mouth which seemed to extend from ear to ear was black or red, in contrast to the color of the cheek. The effect was as if two individual devils, a fiend of fire and a fiend of darkness, had united themselves to form this infernal visage. The stranger grinned in Robin's face, muffled his party-colored features, and was out of sight in a moment.

"Strange things we travelers see!" ejaculated Robin.

He seated himself, however, upon the steps of the church-door, resolving to wait the appointed time for his kinsman. A few moments were consumed in philosophical speculations upon the species of man who had just left him; but having settled this point shrewdly, rationally, and satisfactorily, he was compelled to look elsewhere for his amusement. And first he threw his eyes along the street. It was of more respectable appearance than most of those into which he had wandered, and the moon, creating, like the imaginative power, a beautiful strangeness in familiar objects, gave something of romance to a scene that might not have possessed it in the light of day. The irregular and often quaint architecture of the houses, some of whose roofs were broken into numerous little peaks, while others ascended, steep and narrow, into a single point, and others again were square; the pure snow-white of some of their complexions, the aged darkness of others, and the thousand sparklings, reflected from bright substances in the walls of many; these matters engaged Robin's attention for a while, and then began to grow wearisome. Next he endeavored to define the forms of distant objects, starting away, with almost ghostly indistinctness, just as his eye appeared to grasp them; and finally he took a minute survey of an edifice which stood on the opposite side of the street, directly in front of the church-door, where he was stationed. It was a large, square mansion, distinguished from its neighbors by a balcony, which rested on tall pillars, and by an elaborate Gothic window, communicating therewith.

"Perhaps this is the very house I have been seeking," thought Robin.

Then he strove to speed away the time, by listening to a murmur which swept continually along the street, yet was scarcely audible, except to an unaccustomed ear like his; it was a low, dull, dreamy sound, compounded of many noises, each of which was at too great a distance to be separately heard. Robin marveled at this snore of a sleeping town, and marveled more whenever its continuity was broken by now and then a distant shout, apparently loud where it originated.

But altogether it was a sleep-inspiring sound, and, to shake off its drowsy influence, Robin arose, and climbed a window-frame, that he might view the interior of the church. There the moonbeams came trembling in, and fell down upon the deserted pews, and extended along the quiet aisles. A fainter yet more awful radiance was hovering around the pulpit, and one solitary ray had dared to rest upon the open page of the great Bible. Had nature, in that deep hour, become a worshipper in the house which man had built? Or was that heavenly light the visible sanctity of the place—visible because no earthly and impure feet were within the walls? The scene made Robin's heart shiver with a sensation of loneliness stronger than he had ever felt in the remotest depths of his native woods; so he turned away and sat down again before the door. There were graves around the church, and now an uneasy thought obtruded into Robin's breast. What if the object of his search, which had been so often and so strangely thwarted, were all the time moldering in his shroud? What if his kinsman should glide through yonder gate, and nod and smile to him in dimly passing by?

"Oh, that any breathing thing were here with me!" said Robin.

Recalling his thoughts from this uncomfortable track, he sent them over forest, hill, and stream, and attempted to imagine how that evening of ambiguity and weariness had been spent by his father's household. He pictured them assembled at the door, beneath the tree, the great old tree, which had been spared for its huge twisted trunk, and venerable shade, when a thousand leafy brethren fell. There, at the going down of the summer sun, it was his father's custom to perform domestic worship, that the neighbors might come and join with him like brothers of the family, and that the wayfaring man might pause to drink at that fountain, and keep his heart pure by freshening the memory of home. Robin distinguished the seat of every individual of the little audience; he saw the good man in the midst, holding the Scriptures in the golden light that fell from the western clouds; he beheld him close the book and all rise up to pray. He heard the old thanksgivings for daily mercies, the old supplications for their continuance, to which he had so often listened in weariness, but which were now among his dear remembrances. He perceived the slight inequality of his father's voice when he came to speak of the absent one; he noted how his mother turned her face to the broad and knotted trunk; how his elder brother scorned, because the beard was rough upon his upper lip, to permit his features to be moved; how the younger sister drew down a low hanging branch before her eyes; and how the little one of all, whose sports had hitherto broken the decorum of the scene, understood the prayer for her playmate, and burst into clamorous grief. Then he saw them go in at the door; and when Robin would have entered also, the latch tinkled into its place, and he was excluded from his home.

"Am I here, or there?" cried Robin, starting; for all at

once, when his thoughts had become visible and audible in a dream, the long, wide, solitary street shone out before him.

He aroused himself, and endeavored to fix his attention steadily upon the large edifice which he had surveyed before. But still his mind kept vibrating between fancy and reality; by turns, the pillars of the balcony lengthened into the tall, bare stems of pines, dwindled down to human figures, settled again into their true shape and size, and then commenced a new succession of changes. For a single moment, when he deemed himself awake, he could have sworn that a visage— one which he seemed to remember, yet could not absolutely name as his kinsman's—was looking towards him from the Gothic window. A deeper sleep wrestled with and nearly overcame him, but fled at the sound of footsteps along the opposite pavement. Robin rubbed his eyes, discerned a man passing at the foot of the balcony, and addressed him in a loud, peevish, and lamentable cry.

"Hallo, friend! Must I wait here all night for my kinsman, Major Molineux?"

The sleeping echoes awoke, and answered the voice; and the passenger, barely able to discern a figure sitting in the oblique shade of the steeple, traversed the street to obtain a nearer view. He was himself a gentleman in his prime, of open, intelligent, cheerful, and altogether prepossessing countenance. Perceiving a country youth, apparently homeless and without friends, he accosted him in a tone of real kindness, which had become strange to Robin's ears.

"Well, my good lad, why are you sitting here?" inquired he. "Can I be of service to you in any way?"

"I am afraid not, sir," replied Robin, despondingly; "yet I shall take it kindly if you'll answer me a single question. I've been searching, half the night, for one Major Molineux; now, sir, is there really such a person in these parts, or am I dreaming?"

"Major Molineux! The name is not altogether strange to me," said the gentleman, smiling. "Have you any objection to telling me the nature of your business with him?"

Then Robin briefly related that his father was a clergyman, settled on a small salary, at a long distance back in the country, and that he and Major Molineux were brothers' children. The Major, having inherited riches, and acquired civil and military rank, had visited his cousin, in great pomp, a year or two before; had manifested much interest in Robin and an elder brother, and, being childless himself, had thrown out hints respecting the future establishment of one of them in life. The elder brother was destined to succeed to the farm which his father cultivated in the interval of sacred duties; it was therefore determined that Robin should profit by his kinsman's generous intentions, especially as he seemed to be rather the favorite, and was thought to possess other necessary endowments.

"For I have the name of being a shrewd youth," observed Robin, in this part of his story.

"I doubt not you deserve it," replied his new friend, good-naturedly; "but pray proceed."

"Well, sir, being nearly eighteen years old, and well grown, as you see," continued Robin, drawing himself up to his full height, "I thought it high time to begin the world. So my mother and sister put me in handsome trim, and my father gave me half the remnant of his last year's salary, and five days ago I started for this place, to pay the Major a visit. But, would you believe it, sir! I crossed the ferry a little after dark, and have yet found nobody that would show me the way to his dwelling; only, an hour or two since, I was told to wait here, and Major Molineux would pass by."

"Can you describe the man who told you this?" inquired the gentleman.

"Oh, he was a very ill-favored fellow, sir," replied Robin, "with two great bumps on his forehead, a hook nose, fiery-eyes; and, what struck me as the strangest, his face was of two different colors. Do you happen to know such a man, sir?"

"Not intimately," answered the stranger, "but I chanced to meet him a little time previous to your stopping me. I believe you may trust his word, and that the Major will very shortly pass through this street. In the meantime, as I have a singular curiosity to witness your meeting, I will sit down here upon the steps, and bear you company."

He seated himself accordingly, and soon engaged his companion in animated discourse. It was but of brief continuance, however, for a noise of shouting, which had long been remotely audible, drew so much nearer that Robin inquired its cause.

"What may be the meaning of this uproar?" asked he. "Truly, if your town be always as noisy, I shall find little sleep while I am an inhabitant."

"Why, indeed, friend Robin, there do appear to be three or four riotous fellows abroad tonight," replied the gentleman. "You must not expect all the stillness of your native woods, here in our streets. But the watch will shortly be at the heels of these lads, and—"

"Aye, and set them in the stocks by peep of day," interrupted Robin, recollecting his own encounter with the drowsy lantern-bearer. "But, dear sir, if I may trust my ears, an army of watchmen would never make head against such a multitude of rioters. There were at least a thousand voices went up to make that one shout."

"May not a man have several voices, Robin, as well as two complexions?" said his friend.

"Perhaps a man may; but Heaven forbid that a woman should!" responded the shrewd youth, thinking of the seductive tones of the Major's housekeeper.

The sounds of a trumpet in some neighboring street now became so evident and continual, that Robin's curiosity was strongly excited. In addition to the shouts, he heard frequent bursts from many instruments of discord, and a wild and confused laughter filled up the intervals. Robin rose from the steps, and looked wistfully towards a point whither several people seemed to be hastening.

"Surely some prodigious merry-making is going on,"

exclaimed he. "I have laughed very little since I left home, sir, and should be sorry to lose an opportunity. Shall we step round the corner by that darkish house, and take our share of the fun?"

"Sit down again, sit down, good Robin," replied the gentleman, laying his hand on the skirt of the grey coat. "You forget that we must wait here for your kinsman; and there is reason to believe that he will pass by, in the course of a very few moments."

The near approach of the uproar had now disturbed the neighborhood; windows flew open on all sides; and many heads, in the attire of the pillow, and confused by sleep suddenly broken, were protruded to the gaze of whoever had leisure to observe them. Eager voices hailed each other from house to house, all demanding the explanation, which not a soul could give. Half-dressed men hurried towards the unknown commotion, stumbling as they went over the stone steps that thrust themselves into the narrow foot-walk. The shouts, the laughter, and the tuneless bray, the antipodes of music, came onwards with increasing, din, till scattered individuals, and then denser bodies, began to appear round a corner at the distance of a hundred yards.

"Will you recognize your kinsman, if he passes in this crowd?" inquired the gentleman.

"Indeed, I can't warrant it, sir; but I'll take my stand here, and keep a bright lookout," answered Robin, descending to the outer edge of the pavement.

A mighty stream of people now emptied into the street, and came rolling slowly towards the church. A single horseman wheeled the corner in the midst of them, and close behind him came a band of fearful wind-instruments, sending forth a fresher discord, now that no intervening buildings kept it from the ear. Then a redder light disturbed the moonbeams, and a dense multitude of torches shone along the street, concealing, by their glare, whatever object they illuminated. The single horseman, clad in a military dress, and bearing a drawn sword, rode onward as the leader, and, by his fierce and variegated countenance, appeared like war personified; the red of one cheek was an emblem of fire and sword; the blackness of the other betokened the mourning that attends them. In his train were wild figures in the Indian dress, and many fantastic shapes without a model, giving the whole march a visionary air, as if a dream had broken forth from some feverish brain, and were sweeping visibly through the midnight streets. A mass of people, inactive, except as applauding spectators, hemmed the procession in; and several women ran along the sidewalk, piercing the confusion of heavier sounds with their shrill voices of mirth or terror.

"The double-faced fellow has his eye upon me," muttered Robin, with an indefinite but an uncomfortable idea that he was himself to bear a part in the pageantry.

The leader turned himself in the saddle, and fixed his glance full upon the country youth, as the steed went slowly by. When Robin had freed his eyes from those fiery ones, the musicians were passing before him, and the torches were close at hand; but the unsteady brightness of the latter formed a veil which he could not penetrate. The rattling of wheels over the stones sometimes found its way to his ears, and confused traces of a human form appeared at intervals, and then melted into the vivid light. A moment more, and the leader thundered a command to halt: the trumpets vomited a horrid breath, and then held their peace; the shouts and laughter of the people died away, and there remained only a universal hum, allied to silence. Right before Robin's eyes was an uncovered cart. There the torches blazed the brightest, there the moon shone out like day, and there, in tar-and-feathery dignity, sat his kinsman, Major Molineux!

He was an elderly man, of large and majestic person, and strong, square features, betokening a steady soul; but steady as it was, his enemies had found means to shake it. His face was pale as death, and far more ghastly; the broad forehead was contracted in his agony, so that his eyebrows formed one grizzled line; his eyes were red and wild, and the foam hung white upon his quivering lip. His whole frame was agitated by a quick and continual tremor, which his pride strove to quell, even in those circumstances of overwhelming humiliation. But perhaps the bitterest pang of all was when his eyes met those of Robin; for he evidently knew him on the instant, as the youth stood witnessing the foul disgrace of a head grown grey in honor. They stared at each other in silence, and Robin's knees shook, and his hair bristled, with a mixture of pity and terror. Soon, however, a bewildering excitement began to seize upon his mind; the preceding adventures of the night, the unexpected appearance of the crowd, the torches, the confused din and the hush that followed, the specter of his kinsman reviled by that great multitude, all this, and, more than all, a perception of tremendous ridicule in the whole scene, affected him with a sort of mental inebriety. At that moment a voice of sluggish merriment saluted Robin's ears; he turned instinctively, and just behind the corner of the church stood the lantern-bearer, rubbing his eyes, and drowsily enjoying the lad's amazement. Then he heard a peal of laughter like the ringing of silvery bells; a woman twitched his arm, a saucy eye met his, and he saw the lady of the scarlet petticoat. A sharp, dry cachinnation appealed to his memory, and, standing on tiptoe in the crowd, with his white apron over his head, he beheld the courteous little innkeeper. And lastly, there sailed over the heads of the multitude a great, broad laugh, broken in the midst by two sepulchral hems; thus, "Haw, haw, haw— hem, hem—haw, haw, haw, haw!"

The sound proceeded from the balcony of the opposite edifice, and thither Robin turned his eyes. In front of the Gothic window stood the old citizen, wrapped in a wide gown, his grey periwig exchanged for a nightcap, which was thrust back from his forehead, and his silk stockings hanging about his legs. He supported himself on his polished cane in a fit of convulsive merriment, which manifested itself on his solemn old features like a funny inscription on a tombstone.

Then Robin seemed to hear the voices of the barbers, of the guests of the inn, and of all who had made sport of him that night. The contagion was spreading among the multitude, when, all at once, it seized upon Robin, and he sent forth a shout of laughter that echoed through the street—every man shook his sides, every man emptied his lungs, but Robin's shout was the loudest there. The cloud-spirits peeped from their silvery islands, as the congregated mirth went roaring up the sky! The Man in the Moon heard the far bellow. "Oho," quoth he, "the old earth is frolicsome tonight!"

When there was a momentary calm in that tempestuous sea of sound, the leader gave the sign, the procession resumed its march. On they went, like fiends that throng in mockery around some dead potentate, mighty no more, but majestic still in his agony. On they went, in counterfeited pomp, in senseless uproar, in frenzied merriment, trampling all on an old man's heart. On swept the tumult and left a silent street behind.

* * *

"Well, Robin, are you dreaming?" inquired the gentleman, laying his hand on the youth's shoulder.

Robin started, and withdrew his arm from the stone post to which he had instinctively clung, as the living stream rolled by him. His cheek was somewhat pale, and his eye not quite as lively as in the earlier part of the evening.

"Will you be kind enough to show me the way to the ferry?" said he, after a moment's pause.

"You have, then, adopted a new subject of inquiry?" observed his companion, with a smile.

"Why, yes, sir," replied Robin, rather dryly. "Thanks to you, and to my other friends, I have at last met my kinsman, and he will scarce desire to see my face again. I begin to grow weary of a town life, sir. Will you show me the way to the ferry?"

"No, my good friend Robin—not tonight, at least," said the gentleman. "Some few days hence, if you wish it, I will speed you on your journey. Or, if you prefer to remain with us, perhaps, as you are a shrewd youth, you may rise in the world without the help of your kinsman, Major Molineux."

notes

notes

_____

_____

_____

_____

_____

_____

_____

_____

_____

_____

_____

_____

_____

_____

_____

_____

_____

_____

_____

_____

The Old Regime and the Revolution

ALEXIS DE TOCQUEVILLE

CHAPTER XV: *How the French Sought Reforms Before Liberties*

I have often asked myself what was the source of that passion for political liberty which has inspired the greatest deeds of which mankind can boast. In what feelings does it take root? From whence does it derive nourishment?

I see clearly enough that when a people is badly governed it desires self-government; but this kind of love for independence grows out of certain particular temporary mischiefs wrought by despotism, and is never durable; it passes away with the accident which gave it birth. What seemed to be love for liberty turns out to be mere hatred of a despot. Nations born to freedom hate the intrinsic evil of dependence.

Nor do I believe that a true love for liberty can ever be inspired by the sight of the material advantages it procures, for they are not always clearly visible. It is very true that, in the long run, liberty always yields to those who know how to preserve it comfort, independence, and often wealth; but there are times when it disturbs these blessings for a while, and there are times when their immediate enjoyment can only be secured by a despotism. Those who only value liberty for their sake have never preserved it long.

It is the intrinsic attractions of freedom, its own peculiar charm—quite independently of its incidental benefits—which have seized so strong a hold on the great champions of liberty throughout history; they loved it because they loved the pleasure of being able to speak, to act, to breathe unrestrained, under the sole government of God and the laws. He who seeks freedom for any thing but freedom's self is made to be a slave.

Some nations pursue liberty obstinately through all kinds of dangers and sufferings, not for its material benefits; they deem it so precious and essential a boon that nothing could console them for its loss, while its enjoyment would compensate them for all possible afflictions. Others, on the contrary, grow tired of it in the midst of prosperity; they allow it to be torn from them without resistance rather than compromise the comfort it has bestowed on them by making an effort. What do they need in order to remain free? A taste for freedom. Do not ask me to analyze that sublime taste; it can only be felt. It has a place in every great heart which God has prepared to receive it: it fills and inflames it. To try to explain it to those inferior minds who have never felt it is to waste time.

notes

notes

PART III

Liberty and the Church

The Screwtape Letters

C. S. LEWIS

VIII

My dear Wormwood,

So you "have great hopes that the patient's religious phase is dying away," have you? I always thought the Training College had gone to pieces since they put old Slubgob at the head of it, and now I am sure. Has no one ever told you about the law of Undulation?

Humans are amphibians—half spirit and half animal. (The Enemy's determination to produce such a revolting hybrid was one of the things that determined Our Father to withdraw his support from Him.) As spirits they belong to the eternal world, but as animals they inhabit time. This means that while their spirit can be directed to an eternal object, their bodies, passions, and imaginations are in continual change, for to be in time means to change. Their nearest approach to constancy, therefore, is undulation—the repeated return to a level from which they repeatedly fall back, a series of troughs and peaks. If you had watched your patient carefully you would have seen this undulation in every department of his life—his interest in his work, his affection for his friends, his physical appetites, all go up and down. As long as he lives on earth periods of emotional and bodily richness and liveliness will alternate with periods of numbness and poverty. The dryness and dulness through which your patient is now going are not, as you fondly suppose, your workmanship; they are merely a natural phenomenon which will do us no good unless you make a good use of it.

To decide what the best use of it is, you must ask what use the Enemy wants to make of it, and then do the opposite. Now it may surprise you to learn that in His efforts to get permanent possession of a soul, He relies on the troughs even more than on the peaks; some of His special favourites have gone through longer and deeper troughs than anyone else. The reason is this. To us a human is primarily food; our aim is the absorption of its will into ours, the increase of our own area of selfhood at its expense. But the obedience which the Enemy demands of men is quite a different thing. One must face the fact that all the talk about His love for men, and His service being perfect freedom, is not (as one would gladly believe) mere propaganda, but an appalling truth. He really *does* want to fill the universe with a lot of loathsome little replicas of Himself—creatures whose life, on its miniature scale, will be qualitatively like His own, not because He has absorbed them but because their wills freely conform to His. We want cattle who can finally become food; He wants servants who can finally become sons. We want to suck in, He wants to give out. We are empty and would be filled; He is full and flows over. Our war aim is a world in which Our Father Below has drawn all other beings into himself: the Enemy wants a world full of beings united to Him but still distinct.

And that is where the troughs come in. You must have often wondered why the Enemy does not make more use of His power to be sensibly present to human souls in any degree He chooses and at any moment. But you now see that the Irresistible and the Indisputable are the two weapons which the very nature of His scheme forbids Him to use. Merely to over-ride a human will (as His felt presence in any but the faintest and most mitigated degree would certainly do) would be for Him useless. He cannot ravish. He can only woo. For His ignoble idea is to eat the cake and have it; the creatures are to be one with Him, but yet themselves; merely to cancel them, or assimilate them, will not serve. He is prepared to do a little over-riding at the beginning. He will set them off with communications of His presence which, though faint, seem great to them, with emotional sweetness, and easy conquest over temptation. But He never allows this state of affairs to last long. Sooner or later He withdraws, if not in fact, at least from their conscious experience, all those supports and incentives. He leaves the creature to stand up on its own legs—to carry out from the will alone duties which have lost all relish. It is during such trough periods, much more than during the peak periods, that it is growing into the sort of creature He wants it to be. Hence the prayers offered in the state of dryness are those which please Him best. We can drag our patients along by continual tempting, because we design them only for the table, and the more their will is interfered with the better. He cannot "tempt" to virtue as we do to vice. He wants them to learn to walk and must therefore take away His hand; and if only the will to walk is really there He is pleased even with their stumbles. Do not be deceived, Wormwood. Our cause is never more in danger than when a human, no longer desiring, but still intending, to do our Enemy's will, looks round upon a universe from which every trace of Him seems to have vanished, and asks why he has been forsaken, and still obeys.

But of course the troughs afford opportunities to our side also. Next week I will give you some hints on how to exploit them,

Your affectionate uncle
SCREWTAPE

XV

My dear Wormwood,

I had noticed, of course, that the humans were having a lull in their European war—what they naïvely call "*The War*"!—and am not surprised that there is a corresponding lull in the patient's anxieties. Do we want to encourage this, or to keep him worried? Tortured fear and stupid confidence are both desirable states of mind. Our choice between them raises important questions.

The humans live in time but our Enemy destines them to eternity. He therefore, I believe, wants them to attend chiefly to two things, to eternity itself, and to that point of time which they call the Present. For the Present is the point at which time touches eternity. Of the present moment, and of it only, humans have an experience analogous to the experience which our Enemy has of reality as a whole; in it alone freedom and actuality are offered them. He would therefore have them continually concerned either with eternity (which means being concerned with Him) or with the Present—either meditating on their eternal union with, or separation from, Himself, or else obeying the present voice of conscience, bearing the present cross, receiving the present grace, giving thanks for the present pleasure.

Our business is to get them away from the eternal, and from the Present. With this in view, we sometimes tempt a human (say a widow or a scholar) to live in the Past. But this is of limited value, for they have some real knowledge of the past and it has a determinate nature and, to that extent, resembles eternity. It is far better to make them live in the Future. Biological necessity makes all their passions point in that direction already, so that thought about the Future inflames hope and fear. Also, it is unknown to them, so that in making them think about it we make them think of unrealities. In a word, the Future is, of all things, the thing *least like* eternity. It is the most completely temporal part of time—for the Past is frozen and no longer flows, and the Present is all lit up with eternal rays. Hence the encouragement we have given to all those schemes of thought such as Creative Evolution, Scientific Humanism, or Communism, which fix men's affections on the Future, on the very core of temporality. Hence nearly all vices are rooted in the future. Gratitude looks to the past and love to the present; fear, avarice, lust, and ambition look ahead. Do not think lust an exception. When the present pleasure arrives, the sin (which alone interests us) is already over. The pleasure is just the part of the process which we regret and would exclude if we could do so without losing the sin; it is the part contributed by the Enemy, and therefore experienced in a Present. The sin, which is our contribution, looked forward.

To be sure, the Enemy wants men to think of the Future too—just so much as is necessary for *now* planning the acts of justice or charity which will probably be their duty tomorrow. The duty of planning the morrow's work is *today's* duty;

though its material is borrowed from the future, the duty, like all duties, is in the Present. This is not straw splitting. He does not want men to give the Future their hearts, to place their treasure in it. We do. His ideal is a man who, having worked all day for the good of posterity (if that is his vocation), washes his mind of the whole subject, commits the issue to Heaven, and returns at once to the patience or gratitude demanded by the moment that is passing over him. But we want a man hag-ridden by the Future—haunted by visions of an imminent heaven or hell upon earth—ready to break the Enemy's commands in the present if by so doing we make him think he can attain the one or avert the other—dependent for his faith on the success or failure of schemes whose end he will not live to see. We want a whole race perpetually in pursuit of the rainbow's end, never honest, nor kind, nor happy *now*, but always using as mere fuel wherewith to heap the altar of the future every real gift which is offered them in the Present.

It follows then, in general, and others things being equal, that it is better for your patient to be filled with anxiety or hope (it doesn't much matter which) about this war than for him to be living in the present. But the phrase "living in the present" is ambiguous. It may describe a process which is really just as much concerned with the Future as anxiety itself. Your man may be untroubled about the Future, not because he is concerned with the Present, but because he has persuaded himself that the Future is going to be agreeable. As long as that is the real course of his tranquillity, his tranquillity will do us good, because it is only piling up more disappointment, and therefore more impatience, for him when his false hopes are dashed. If, on the other hand, he is aware that horrors may be in store for him and is praying for the virtues, wherewith to meet them, and meanwhile concerning himself with the Present because there, and there alone, all duty, all grace, all knowledge, and all pleasure dwell, his state is very undesirable and should be attacked at once. Here again, our Philological Arm has done good work; try the word "complacency" on him. But, of course, it is most likely that he is "living in the Present" for none of these reasons but simply because his health is good and he is enjoying his work. The phenomenon would then be merely natural. All the same, I should break it up if I were you. No natural phenomenon is really in our favour. And anyway, why *should* the creature be happy?

Your affectionate uncle
SCREWTAPE

notes

notes

Veritatis Splendor

POPE ST. JOHN PAUL II

CHAPTER II: "DO NOT BE CONFORMED TO THIS WORLD" (ROM. 12:2)

The Church and the discernment of certain tendencies in present-day moral theology

> *"You will know the truth,*
> *and the truth will make you free."* (JN. 8:32)

31. The human issues most frequently debated and differently resolved in contemporary moral reflection are all closely related, albeit in various ways, to a crucial issue: *human freedom*.

Certainly people today have a particularly strong sense of freedom. As the Council's Declaration on Religious Freedom *Dignitatis Humanae* had already observed, "the dignity of the human person is a concern of which people of our time are becoming increasingly more aware."[1] Hence the insistent demand that people be permitted to "enjoy the use of their own responsible judgment and freedom, and decide on their actions on grounds of duty and conscience, without external pressure or coercion."[2] In particular, the right to religious freedom and to respect for conscience on its journey towards the truth is increasingly perceived as the foundation of the cumulative rights of the person.[3]

This heightened sense of the dignity of the human person and of his or her uniqueness, and of the respect due to the journey of conscience, certainly represents one of the positive achievements of modern culture. This perception, authentic as it is, has been expressed in a number of more or less adequate ways, some of which however diverge from the truth about man as a creature and the image of God, and thus need to be corrected and purified in the light of faith.[4]

---

1. Second Vatican Ecumenical Council, Declaration on Religious Freedom *Dignitatis Humanae*, 1, referring to John XXIII, Encyclical Letter *Pacem in Terris* (April 11, 1963): *AAS* 55 (1963), 279; ibid., 265, and to Pius XII, *Radio Message* (December 24, 1944): *AAS* 37 (1945), 14.
2. *Dignitatis Humanae*, 1.
3. Cf. Encyclical Letter *Redemptor Hominis* (March 4, 1979), 17: *AAS* 71 (1979), 295–300; Address to the Fifth International Colloquium of Juridical Studies (March 10, 1984), 4; *Insegnamenti* VII, 1 (1984), 656; Congregation for the Doctrine of the Faith, Instruction on Christian Freedom and Liberation *Libertatis Conscientia* (March 22, 1986),19: *AAS* 79 (1987), 561.
4. Cf. Second Vatican Ecumenical Council, Pastoral Constitution on the Church in the Modern World *Gaudium et Spes*, 11.

32. Certain currents of modern thought have gone so far as to *exalt freedom to such an extent that it becomes an absolute, which would then be the source of values.* This is the direction taken by doctrines which have lost the sense of the transcendent or which are explicitly atheist. The individual conscience is accorded the status of a supreme tribunal of moral judgment which hands down categorical and infallible decisions about good and evil. To the affirmation that one has a duty to follow one's conscience is unduly added the affirmation that one's moral judgment is true merely by the fact that it has its origin in the conscience. But in this way the inescapable claims of truth disappear, yielding their place to a criterion of sincerity, authenticity and "being at peace with oneself," so much so that some have come to adopt a radically subjectivistic conception of moral judgment.

As is immediately evident, *the crisis of truth* is not unconnected with this development. Once the idea of a universal truth about the good, knowable by human reason, is lost, inevitably the notion of conscience also changes. Conscience is no longer considered in its primordial reality as an act of a person's intelligence, the function of which is to apply the universal knowledge of the good in a specific situation and thus to express a judgment about the right conduct to be chosen here and now. Instead, there is a tendency to grant to the individual conscience the prerogative of independently determining the criteria of good and evil and then acting accordingly. Such an outlook is quite congenial to an individualist ethic, wherein each individual is faced with his own truth, different from the truth of others. Taken to its extreme consequences, this individualism leads to a denial of the very idea of human nature.

These different notions are at the origin of currents of thought which posit a radical opposition between moral law and conscience, and between nature and freedom.

33. *Side by side* with its exaltation of freedom, yet oddly in contrast with it, *modern culture radically questions the very existence of this freedom.* A number of disciplines, grouped under the name of the "behavioural sciences," have rightly drawn attention to the many kinds of psychological and social conditioning which influence the exercise of human freedom. Knowledge of these conditionings and the study they have received represent important achievements which have found application in various areas, for example in pedagogy or the administration of justice. But some people, going beyond the conclusions which can be legitimately drawn from these observations, have come to question or even deny the very reality of human freedom.

Mention should also be made here of theories which misuse scientific research about the human person. Arguing from the great variety of customs, behaviour patterns and institutions present in humanity, these theories end up, if not with an outright denial of universal human values, at least with a relativistic conception of morality.

34. "Teacher, what good must I do to have eternal life?" *The question of morality*, to which Christ provides the answer, *cannot prescind from the issue of freedom. Indeed, it considers that issue central*, for there can be no morality without freedom: "It is only in freedom that man can turn to what is good."[5] *But what sort of freedom?* The Council, considering our contemporaries who "highly regard" freedom and "assiduously pursue" it, but who "often cultivate it in wrong ways as a licence to do anything they please, even evil," speaks of *"genuine" freedom*: "Genuine freedom is an outstanding manifestation of the divine image in man. For God willed to leave man "in the power of his own counsel" (cf. Sir. 15:14), so that he would seek his Creator of his own accord and would freely arrive at full and blessed perfection by cleaving to God."[6] Although each individual has a right to be respected in his own journey in search of the truth, there exists a prior moral obligation, and a grave one at that, to seek the truth and to adhere to it once it is known.[7] As Cardinal John Henry Newman, that outstanding defender of the rights of conscience, forcefully put it: "Conscience has rights because it has duties."[8]

5. Ibid., 17.
6. Ibid.
7. Cf. *Dignitatis Humanae*, 2; cf. also Gregory XVI, Encyclical Epistle *Mirari Vos Arbitramur* (August 15, 1832): *Acta Gregorii Papae* XVI, I, 169–174; Pius IX, Encyclical Epistle *Quanta Cura* (December 8, 1864): *Pii IX P.M. Acta*, I, 3, 687–700; Leo XIII, Encyclical Letter *Libertas Praestantissimum* (June 20, 1888): *Leonis XIII P.M. Acta*, VIII (Rome, 1889), 212–246.
8. *A Letter Addressed to His Grace the Duke of Norfolk: Certain Difficulties Felt by Anglicans in Catholic Teaching* (London: Longman, Green and Company, 1868–1881), vol. 2, p. 250.

Certain tendencies in contemporary moral theology, under the influence of the currents of subjectivism and individualism just mentioned, involve novel interpretations of the relationship of freedom to the moral law, human nature and conscience, and propose novel criteria for the moral evaluation of acts. Despite their variety, these tendencies are at one in lessening or even denying *the dependence of freedom on truth.*

If we wish to undertake a critical discernment of these tendencies—a discernment capable of acknowledging what is legitimate, useful and of value in them, while at the same time pointing out their ambiguities, dangers and errors—we must examine them in the light of the fundamental dependence of freedom upon truth, a dependence which has found its clearest and most authoritative expression in the words of Christ: "You will know the truth, and the truth will set you free" (Jn. 8:32).

CHAPTER III: "LEST THE CROSS OF CHRIST BE EMPTIED OF ITS POWER" (1 COR. 1:17)

Moral good for the life of the Church and of the world

"For freedom Christ has set us free." (Gal 5:1)

84. The *fundamental question* which the moral theories mentioned above pose in a particularly forceful way is that of the relationship of man's freedom to God's law; it is ultimately the question of the *relationship between freedom and truth.*

According to Christian faith and the Church's teaching, "only the freedom which submits to the Truth leads the human person to his true good. The good of the person is to be in the Truth and to *do* the Truth."[9]

A comparison between the Church's teaching and today's social and cultural situation immediately makes clear the urgent need *for the Church herself to develop an intense pastoral effort precisely with regard to this fundamental question.* "This essential bond between Truth, the Good and Freedom has been largely lost sight of by present-day culture. As a result, helping man to rediscover it represents nowadays one of the specific requirements of the Church's mission, for the salvation

---

9.   Address to the International Congress of Moral Theology (April 10, 1986), 1; *Insegnamenti* IX, 1 (1986), 970.

of the world. Pilate's question: "What is truth" reflects the distressing perplexity of a man who often no longer knows *who he is, whence* he comes and *where* he is going. Hence we not infrequently witness the fearful plunging of the human person into situations of gradual self-destruction. According to some, it appears that one no longer need acknowledge the enduring absoluteness of any moral value. All around us we encounter contempt for human life after conception and before birth; the ongoing violation of basic rights of the person; the unjust destruction of goods minimally necessary for a human life. Indeed, something more serious has happened: man is no longer convinced that only in the truth can he find salvation. The saving power of the truth is contested, and freedom alone, uprooted from any objectivity, is left to decide by itself what is good and what is evil. This relativism becomes, in the field of theology, a lack of trust in the wisdom of God, who guides man with the moral law. Concrete situations are unfavourably contrasted with the precepts of the moral law, nor is it any longer maintained that, when all is said and done, the law of God is always the one true good of man."[10]

85. The discernment which the Church carries out with regard to these ethical theories is not simply limited to denouncing and refuting them. In a positive way, the Church seeks, with

10.   Ibid., 2; *Insegnamenti* IX, 1, 970–971.

great love, to help all the faithful to form a moral conscience which will make judgments and lead to decisions in accordance with the truth, following the exhortation of the Apostle Paul: "Do not be conformed to this world but be transformed by the renewal of your mind, that you may prove what is the will of God, what is good and acceptable and perfect" (Rom. 12:2). This effort by the Church finds its support— the "secret" of its educative power—not so much in doctrinal statements and pastoral appeals to vigilance, as in *constantly looking to the Lord Jesus.* Each day the Church looks to Christ with unfailing love, fully aware that the true and final answer to the problem of morality lies in him alone. In a particular way, it is *in the Crucified Christ* that *the Church finds the answer* to the question troubling so many people today: how can obedience to universal and unchanging moral norms respect the uniqueness and individuality of the person, and not represent a threat to his freedom and dignity? The Church makes her own the Apostle Paul's awareness of the mission he had received: "Christ...sent me...to preach the Gospel, and not with eloquent wisdom, lest the cross of Christ be emptied of its power.... We preach Christ crucified, a stumbling block to Jews and folly to Gentiles, but to those who are called, both Jews and Greeks, Christ the power of God and the wisdom of God" (1 Cor. 1:17, 23–24). *The Crucified Christ reveals the authentic meaning of freedom; he lives it fully in the total gift of himself* and calls his disciples to share in his freedom.

86. Rational reflection and daily experience demonstrate the weakness which marks man's freedom. That freedom is real but limited: its absolute and unconditional origin is not in itself, but in the life within which it is situated and which represents for it, at one and the same time, both a limitation and a possibility. Human freedom belongs to us as creatures; it is a freedom which is given as a gift, one to be received like a seed and to be cultivated responsibly. It is an essential part of that creaturely image which is the basis of the dignity of the person. Within that freedom there is an echo of the primordial vocation whereby the Creator calls man to the true Good, and even more, through Christ's Revelation, to become his friend and to share his own divine life. It is at once inalienable self-possession and openness to all that exists, in passing beyond self to knowledge and love of the other.[11] Freedom then is rooted in the truth about man, and it is ultimately directed towards communion.

Reason and experience not only confirm the weakness of human freedom; they also confirm its tragic aspects. Man comes to realize that his freedom is in some mysterious way inclined to betray this openness to the True and the Good, and that all too often he actually prefers to choose finite, limited and ephemeral goods. What is more, within his errors and negative decisions, man glimpses the source of a deep

---

11. Cf. Second Vatican Ecumenical Council, Pastoral Constitution on the Church in the Modern World *Gaudium et Spes*, 24.

rebellion, which leads him to reject the Truth and the Good in order to set himself up as an absolute principle unto himself: "You will be like God" (Gen. 3:5). Consequently, *freedom itself needs to be set free*. It is Christ who sets it free: he "has set us free for freedom" (cf. Gal. 5:1).

87. Christ reveals, first and foremost, that the frank and open acceptance of truth is the condition for authentic freedom: "You will know the truth, and the truth will set you free" (Jn. 8:32).[12] This is truth which sets one free in the face of worldly power and which gives the strength to endure martyrdom. So it was with Jesus before Pilate: "For this I was born, and for this I have come into the world, to bear witness to the truth" (Jn. 18:37). The true worshippers of God must thus worship him "in spirit and truth" (Jn. 4:23): *in this worship they become free*. Worship of God and a relationship with truth are revealed in Jesus Christ as the deepest foundation of freedom.

Furthermore, Jesus reveals by his whole life, and not only by his words, that freedom is acquired in *love*, that is, in the *gift of self*. The one who says: "Greater love has no man than this, that a man lay down his life for his friends" (Jn. 15:13), freely goes out to meet his Passion (cf. Mt. 26:46), and in obedience to the Father gives his life on the Cross for all men (cf. Phil. 2:6–11). Contemplation of Jesus Crucified

---

12. Cf. Encyclical Letter *Redemptor Hominis* (March 4, 1979), 12: *AAS* 71 (1979), 280–281.

is thus the highroad which the Church must tread every day if she wishes to understand the full meaning of freedom: the gift of self in *service to God and one's brethren*. Communion with the Crucified and Risen Lord is the never-ending source from which the Church draws unceasingly in order to live in freedom, to give of herself and to serve. Commenting on the verse in Psalm 100, "Serve the Lord with gladness," Saint Augustine says: "In the house of the Lord, slavery is free. It is free because it serves not out of necessity, but out of charity... Charity should make you a servant, just as truth has made you free...you are at once both a servant and free: a servant, because you have become such; free, because you are loved by God your Creator; indeed, you have also been enabled to love your Creator... You are a servant of the Lord and you are a freedman of the Lord. Do not go looking for a liberation which will lead you far from the house of your liberator!"[13]

The Church, and each of her members, is thus called to share in the *munus regale* of the Crucified Christ (cf. Jn. 12:32), to share in the grace and in the responsibility of the Son of man who came "not to be served but to serve, and to give his life as a ransom for many" (Mt. 20:28).[14]

Jesus, then, is the living, personal summation of perfect freedom in total obedience to the will of God. His crucified flesh fully reveals the unbreakable bond between freedom and

13. *Enarratio in Psalmum XCIX*, 7: *CCL* 39, 1397.
14. Cf. *Lumen Gentium* 36; cf. *Redemptor Hominis*, 21: *AAS* 71 (1979), 316–317.

truth, just as his Resurrection from the dead is the supreme exaltation of the fruitfulness and saving power of a freedom lived out in truth.

THE BLESSINGS OF LIBERTY

notes

notes

Leisure, the Basis of Culture

JOSEF PIEPER

IV

In the foregoing sections leisure was tentatively defined and outlined in its ideal form. It now remains to consider the problem of realizing its "hopes," of its latent powers of gaining acceptance, and its possible impetus in history. The practical problem involved might be stated thus: Is it possible, from now on, to maintain and defend, or even to reconquer, the right and claims of leisure, in face of the claims of "total labor" that are invading every sphere of life? Leisure, it must be remembered, is not a Sunday afternoon idyll, but the preserve of freedom, of education and culture, and of that undiminished humanity which views the world as a whole. In other words, is it going to be possible to save men from becoming officials and functionaries and "workers" to the exclusion of all else? Can that possibly be done, and if so in what circumstances? There is no doubt of one thing: the world of the "worker" is taking shape with dynamic force—with such a velocity that, rightly or wrongly, one is tempted to speak of demonic force in history.

The attempt to withstand this invasion has been made at a number of different points for some time past. It is even possible to lay down that certain forms of opposition are inadequate; for example the position—quite legitimate up to a point—called "art for art's sake," was an attempt to isolate the realm of art from the universal utilitarianism that seeks to turn everything in the world to some useful purpose. In our own day the real historical fronts still remain to some extent fluid, masked by backward-looking interim solutions. Among these are the return to "tradition" pure and simple; an emphasis on our duty as the heirs of classical antiquity; the struggle to retain the classics in the schools and the "academic" (philosophical) character of the universities—in a word *humanism*. Such are the designations of some of the positions from which a threatened and endangered body aspires to defend itself.

The question is whether these positions will be held and in fact whether they *can* be held. The problem is whether "Humanism" is an adequate watchword—adequate, not simply as a psychologically good rallying cry, as an effective summons to battle, but as a conception metaphysically sound and therefore ultimately credible, in the sense of providing a genuine source of power capable of influencing the course of history. ("Humanism," it should here be observed, has recently made its appearance in Eastern Germany, where it has become the fashion to speak of economic materialism as "humanistic"; and in France, an atheistic existentialism also claims to be humanistic—neither usage, what is more, is entirely without justification!) The real question is therefore, whether an appeal to "humanism" is adequate—in face of the totalitarian claims of the world of work.

Before we attempt an answer to this question, we must clear away a number of obvious misunderstandings, which have no doubt already arisen, by saying something about the social aspect of our problem. This is the reason for our excursus on the proletariat and deproletarianization.

Excursus on the Proletariat and Deproletarianization

It has already been explained that the term "intellectual worker" adds pointed expression to the claims of the world of work. But a modern German dictionary (Trübner's) maintains, on the contrary, that the relatively modern terms "intellectual work," "intellectual worker" are valuable because "they do away with the age-old distinction, still further emphasized in modern times, between the manual worker and the educated man."[1] Now, if that designation is *not* accepted, or at least only with reservations, it surely implies a certain

---

1. Trübner's *Deutsches Worterbuch* (Berlin, 1939).

conception of those social contrasts? The refusal to allow the validity of the term "intellectual worker" certainly means one thing: it means that the common denominator "work" and "worker" is not considered a proper or a possible basis upon which to bridge the contrast of the classes of society. But does it not mean something more? Does it not mean that the gulf between an educated class which is free to pursue knowledge as an end in itself, and the proletarian who knows nothing beyond the spare time which is barely sufficient for him to renew his strength for his daily work—does it not mean logically, from our point of view, that this gulf is in fact necessarily deepened and widened, independently of whatever subjective views and intentions may be at work? This objection is not to be taken lightly.

Indeed, on one occasion Plato contrasts the figure of the philosopher with that of the *bánausos*, the common working man. Philosophers are those

> who have not grown up like serfs, but in quite different, not to say contrary, circumstances. Now this, O Theodorus, is the way of each one individually: the one whom you call a philosopher, is truly brought up in freedom and leisure, and goes unpunished though he seems simple and useless when it is a matter of menial offices, even though he should not, for instance, know how to tie up a parcel that has to be sent on, or how to prepare a tasty dish...; the other way is the way of those who know,

indeed, how to perform all these things well and smartly, but on the other hand do not even know how to wear their cloak like a gentleman, and still less how to prize the good life of gods and men in harmonious phrases.

This passage is to be found in Plato's *Theaetetus*.[2] It is to be noted that the Greek conception of the *bánausos* (the common working man)—as might easily be shown from the above quotation from Plato, means not only an uneducated man, a man insensitive to poetry and art, and with no spiritual view of the world, but furthermore a man who lives by manual labor as distinguished from the man who owns sufficient property to dispose freely of his time. Here, once again, does it not appear as though our thesis implied a return to the Greek notion of the common working man and to the social and educational conceptions of the pre-Christian era? Certainly not! Yet is this not implicit in the refusal to accept the term "work" (which, as has always been said, is supposed to be a term of praise) as applying to the *whole* sphere of man's intellectual and spiritual activity? On the contrary, in my opinion everything must be done, on the one hand to obliterate a contrast of this kind between the classes, but on the other hand it is quite wrong, and indeed foolish, to attempt to achieve that aim by looking for social unity in what is (for the moment!) the purely terminological reduction of the educated stratum to proletarian

2.   *Theaetetus*, 175f.

level, instead of the real abolition of the proletariat. What do we mean, fundamentally, by the words "proletariat," and "deproletarianization"?—It will be as well, in attempting to answer the question and to define the terms, to leave firmly aside all discussion of the practicability of "deproletarianizing," in order to answer the question purely "theoretically" and from the point of view of the principles involved.

In the first place, a proletarian and a poor man are not the same. A man may be poor without being a proletarian: a beggar in medieval society was certainly not a proletarian. Equally, a proletarian is not necessarily poor: a mechanic, a "specialist" or a "technician" in a "totalitarian work state" is certainly a proletarian. Secondly, this, though obvious, has to be said: the negative aspect of the notion "proletariat," the thing to be got rid of, does not consist in the fact that it is a condition limited to a particular stratum of society; so that the negative aspect would disappear once *all* had become proletarians. "Proletarianism" cannot obviously be overcome by making everyone proletarian.

What, then, is proletarianism? If the numerous sociological definitions and terms are reduced to a common denominator, the result might be expressed in the following terms: the proletarian is the man who is fettered to the process of work.

This still leaves the phrase "process of work" vague and in need of clarification. It does not, of course, mean work in the ordinary sense: the never-ceasing activity of man. "Process of work," here, means useful work in the sense already defined, of contributing to the general need, to the *bonum utile*. And so "process of work" means the all-embracing process in which things are used for the sake of the public need. To be fettered to work means to be bound to this vast utilitarian process in which our needs are satisfied, and, what is more, tied to such an extent that the life of the working man is wholly consumed in it.

To be tied in this way may be the result of various causes. The cause may be lack of property: everyone who is a propertyless wage-earner is a proletarian, everyone "who owns nothing but his power to work,"[3] and who is consequently compelled to sell his capacity to work, is a proletarian. But to be tied to work may also be caused by coercion in a totalitarian state; in such a state everyone, whether propertied or unpropertied, is a proletarian because he is bound by the orders of others "to the necessities of an absolute economic process of production,"[4] by outside forces, which means that he is entirely subject to economic forces, is a proletarian.

In the third place, to be tied to the process of work may be ultimately due to the inner impoverishment of the individual: in this context everyone whose life is completely filled by his work (in the special sense of the word work) is a proletarian because his life has shrunk inwardly, and contracted, with the

---

3. Pius XI, Encyclical *Quadragesimo anno*.
4. Ibid.

result that he can no longer act significantly outside his work, and perhaps can no longer even conceive of such a thing.

Finally, all these different forms of proletarianism, particularly the last two, mutually attract one another and in so doing intensify each other. The "total work" State needs the spiritually impoverished, one-track mind of the "functionary"; and he, in his turn, is naturally inclined to find complete satisfaction in his "service" and thereby achieves the illusion of a life fulfilled, which he acknowledges and willingly accepts.

This inner constraint, the inner chains which fetter us to "work," prompts a further question: "proletarianism" thus understood, is perhaps a symptomatic state of mind common to *all* levels of society and by no means confined to the "proletariat," to the "worker," a *general* symptom that is merely found isolated in unusually acute form in the proletariat; so that it might be asked whether we are not all of us proletarians and all of us, consequently, ripe and ready to fall into the hands of some collective labor State and be at its disposal as functionaries—even though explicitly of the contrary political opinion. In that case, spiritual immunization against the seductive appeal and the power of totalitarian forms must, surely, be sought and hoped for at a much deeper level of thought than on the level of purely political considerations?[5]

---

5. Although in writing *Thesen zur sozialen Politik* (first published in 1933), I *expressly* limited myself to the consideration of political questions, and was therefore aware of the limitations of a purely political view, I now regard the essay as requiring completion at many points. It is surely characteristic of the generation formed between the wars that they expected in general too much from unadulterated politics.

Leisure, the Basis of Culture

In this context the distinction between the liberal and the servile arts acquires a fresh significance. In antiquity and the Middle Ages, the essence of the *artes serviles* was held to consist in their being directed, as St. Thomas says, "to the satisfaction of a need through activity." "Proletarianism" would then mean the limitation of existence and activity to the sphere of the *artes serviles*—whether this limitation were occasioned by lack of property, State compulsion, or spiritual impoverishment. By the same token, "deproletarianizing" would mean: enlarging the scope of life beyond the confines of merely useful servile work, and widening the sphere of servile work to the advantage of the liberal arts; and this process, once again, can only be carried out by combining three things: by giving the wage-earner the opportunity to save and acquire property, by limiting the power of the state, and by overcoming the inner impoverishment of the individual.

The phrase "servile work" strikes contemporary ears as extremely offensive—that is well known. Nevertheless, it would be a dangerous procedure to attempt to deny the "servility" of work. By setting up the fiction that work does *not* "serve" primarily for some purpose outside itself, we accomplish precisely the opposite of what we intended or pretended to accomplish. By no means do we "liberate" or "rehabilitate" the laboring man. Instead, we establish precisely that inhuman state characteristic of labor under totalitarianism: the ultimate tying of the worker to production. For the process of production itself is understood and proclaimed as the activity that gives meaning to human existence.

Genuine deproletarianization, which must not be confounded with the struggle against poverty (there is no need to waste words on the vital importance of *that*), assumes that the distinction between the *artes liberales* and the *artes serviles* is a meaningful one, that is, it must be recognized that there is a real distinction between useful activity on the one hand, the sense and purpose of which is not in itself, and on the other hand the liberal arts which cannot be put at the disposal of useful ends. And it is entirely consistent that those who stand for the "proletarianizing" of everyone, should deny all meaning to the distinction and try to prove that it has no basis in reality.

To take an example: the distinction between the liberal arts and the servile arts runs parallel with the terms: honorarium and wage. Properly speaking, the liberal arts receive an honorarium, while servile work receives a wage. The concept of honorarium implies that an incommensurability exists between performance and recompense, and that the performance cannot "really" be recompensed. Wages, on the other hand (in the extreme sense in which they differ from an honorarium), are intended as payment for the specific work performed, without consideration of the needs of the worker. It is significant that those members of the intelligentsia who are imbued with "working-class" ideals refuse to recognize this distinction between honorarium and wages. To their minds, only wages exist. In a sort of manifesto on the situation of the writer in society today,[6] in which literature is proclaimed a "social function," Jean-Paul Sartre announces that the writer, who has in the past so seldom "established a relation between his work and its material recompense," must learn to regard himself as "a worker who receives the reward of his effort." There, the incommensurability between the achievement and the reward, as it is implied and expressed in an "honorarium," is declared nonexistent even in the field of philosophy and poetry which are, on the contrary, simply "intellectual work." By contrast a social doctrine steeped in the tradition of Christian Europe would not only hold firmly to the distinction between an honorarium and a wage, it would not only hesitate to regard every reward as a wage; it would go further and would even maintain that there is no such thing as a recompense for a thing done which did not retain in some degree the character (whether much or little) of an honorarium, for even "servile" work cannot be entirely equated with the material recompense because it is a "human" action, so that it always retains something incommensurable with the recompense—just like the liberal arts.

And so it comes about, paradoxical though it may seem, that the proletarian dictator Stalin should say: "The worker must be paid according to the work done and not according to his needs,"[7] and that the encyclical *Quadragesimo anno* which

---

6. Published in the first number of *Les Temps Modernes*.
7. Joseph Stalin in a public statement made in 1933.

has for one of its principal aims the "deproletarianizing" of the masses, should assert that "in the first place the worker has the right to a wage sufficient to support himself and his family."[8] On the one hand, there is an attempt to restrict and even to extirpate the liberal arts: it is alleged that only useful, "paying" work makes sense; on the other hand, there is an attempt to extend the character of "liberal art" deep down into every human action, even the humblest servile work. The former aims at making all men into proletarians, the latter at "deproletarianizing" the masses.

There is, however, a fact which from the vantage-point we have now reached must be strikingly clear and significant, and it is this: whereas the "total work" State declares all un-useful work "undesirable," and even expropriates free time in the service of work, there is one Institution in the world which forbids useful activity, and servile work, on particular days, and in this way prepares, as it were, a sphere for a non-proletarian existence.

Thus one of the first socialists, P. J. Proudhon (whom Marx dismissed as a "petit bourgeois")[9] was not so far wrong in beginning his work with a pamphlet on the celebration of Sunday, the social significance of which he expresses in the following words: "On one day in the week servants regained

8. *Quadragesimo anno*, 55ff.
9. P. J. Proudhon, *Die Sonntagsfeier, aus deni Gesichtspunkt des öffentlichen Gesund-heitswesens, der Moral, der Familien- und bürgerlichen Ver hältnisse betrachtet* (Kassel, 1850).

the dignity of human beings, and stood again on a level with their masters."[10] And in the introduction to his little book, Proudhon gets very near to the heart of the matter when he says, "Discussion about work and wages, organization and industry, which is so rife at present ought, it seems to me, to start with the study of a law which would have as its basis a theory of rest."[11] It is true that the full meaning of this "theory of rest" is not open to one who, like Proudhon, examines it exclusively "from the point of view of public health, morality, the family and social conditions." And here is something to be examined more closely.

Let us begin by summing up what has already been said in this excursus: If the essence of "proletarian" is the fact of being fettered to the process of work, then the central problem of liberating men from this condition lies in making a whole field of significant activity available and open to the working man—of activity which is *not* "work"; in other words: in making the sphere of real leisure available to him.

This end cannot be attained by purely political measures and by widening and, in that sense, "freeing" the life of the individual economically. Although this would entail much that is necessary, the essential would still be wanting. The provision of an external opportunity for leisure is not enough; it can only be fruitful if the man himself is capable of leisure

10. Ibid., p. 18.
11. Ibid., p. vi.

and can, as we say, "occupy his leisure," or (as the Greeks still more clearly say) *skolen agein*, "work his leisure" (this usage brings out very clearly the by no means "leisurely" character of leisure).

"That is the principal point: with what kind of activity is man to occupy his leisure"[12]—who would suspect that that was a sentence taken from a book more than two thousand years old, none other than the *Politics* of Aristotle? What, then, ultimately makes leisure inwardly possible and, at the same time, what is its real justification?

12. Aristotle, *Politics*, 8, 3 (1337b).

V

WHAT, then, ultimately makes leisure inwardly possible and, at the same time, what is its fundamental justification?

In posing this question we are asking again: Can the realm of leisure be saved and its foundations upheld by an appeal to *humanism?* On closer inspection it will be seen that "humanism," understood as a mere appeal to a *humanum*, does not serve.

The soul of leisure, it can be said, lies in "celebration." Celebration is the point at which the three elements of leisure come to a focus: relaxation, effortlessness, and superiority of "active leisure" to all functions.

But if celebration is the core of leisure, then leisure can only be made possible and justifiable on the same basis as the celebration of a festival. *That basis is divine worship.*

THE meaning of celebration, we have said, is man's affirmation of the universe and his experiencing the world in an aspect other than its everyday one. Now we cannot conceive a more intense affirmation of the world than "praise of God," praise of the Creator of this very world. This statement is generally received with a discomfort formed of many elements—I have often witnessed that. But its truth is irrefutable. The most festive festival it is possible to celebrate is divine worship. And there is no festival that does not draw its vitality from worship and that has not become a festival by virtue of its origin in worship. There is no such thing as a festival "without gods"— whether it be a carnival or a marriage. That is not a demand, or a requirement; it does not mean that that is how things ought to be. Rather, it is meant as a simple statement of fact: however dim the recollection of the association may have become in men's minds, a feast "without gods," and unrelated to worship, is quite simply unknown. It is true that ever since the French Revolution attempts have repeatedly been made to manufacture feast days and holidays that have no connection with divine worship, or are sometimes even opposed to it: "Brutus days," or even that hybrid, "Labor Day." In point of fact the stress and strain of giving them some kind of festal appearance is one of the very best proofs of the significance of divine worship for a feast; and nothing illustrates so clearly that festivity is only possible where divine worship is still a vital act—and nothing shows this so clearly as a comparison between a living and deeply traditional feast day, with its roots in divine worship, and one of those rootless celebrations, carefully and unspontaneously prepared beforehand, and as artificial as a maypole.

Certainly we must ask whether the great epoch of artificial festivals is not still to come. Perhaps we should be preparing ourselves for it. Might we not expect the forces of society or, in the extreme case, the holders of political power to lavish tremendous effort on specious arrangements for the sake of artificially engendering a sham festivity—an illusory, semi-opaque semblance of "holidays" that would be devoid of the true and ultimate affirmation of the world that is the essence of the festive. Such holidays, moreover, are in fact based on suppression of such affirmation; they derive their dangerous seductiveness precisely from that.

What is true of celebration is true of leisure: its possibility, its ultimate justification derive from its roots in divine worship. That is not a conceptual abstraction, but the simple truth as may be seen from the history of religion. What does a "day of rest" mean in the Bible, and for that matter in Greece and Rome? To rest from work means that time is reserved for divine worship: certain days and times are set aside and transferred to "the exclusive property of the gods."[13]

Divine worship means the same thing where time is concerned, as the temple where space is concerned. "Temple" means (as may be seen from the original sense of the word): that a particular piece of ground is specially reserved, and marked off from the remainder of the land which is used either for agriculture or for habitation. And this plot of land is transferred to the estate of the gods, it is neither lived on, nor cultivated. And similarly in divine worship a certain definite space of *time* is set aside from working hours and days, a limited time, specially marked off—and like the space allotted to the temple, is not *used*, is withdrawn from all merely utilitarian ends. Every seventh day is such a period of time. It is the "festival time," and it arises in this way and no other.

---

13.   *Reallexikon für Antike mid Christentum,* 1942 Article "Arbeitsruhe."

There can be no such thing in the world of "total labor"
as space which is not used *on principle*; no such thing as a plot
of ground, or a period of time withdrawn from use. There is
in fact no *room* in the world of "total labor" either for divine
worship, or for a feast: because the "worker's" world, the
world of "labor" rests solely upon the principle of rational
utilization. A "feast day" in that world is either a pause in
the midst of work (and for the sake of work, of course), or in
the case of "Labor Day," or whatever feast days of the world
of "work" may be called, it is the very principle of work that
is being celebrated—once again, work stops for the sake of
work, and the feast is subordinated to "work." There can of
course be games, *circenses*, circuses—but who would think of
describing that kind of mass entertainment as festal?

It simply cannot be otherwise: the world of "work" and
of the "worker" is a poor, impoverished world, be it ever so
rich in material goods; for on an exclusively utilitarian basis,
on the basis, that is, of the world of "work," genuine wealth,
wealth which implies overflowing into superfluities, into
unnecessaries, is just not possible. Wherever the superfluous
makes its appearance it is immediately subjected to the ratio-
nalist, utilitarian principle of the world of work. And, as the
traditional Russian saying puts it: work does not make one
rich, but round-shouldered.

On the other hand, divine worship, of its very nature, creates a sphere of real wealth and superfluity, even in the midst
of the direst material want—because sacrifice is the living

heart of worship. And what does sacrifice mean? It means a voluntary offering freely given. It definitely does not involve utility; it is in fact absolutely antithetic to utility. Thus, the act of worship creates a store of real wealth that cannot be consumed by the workaday world. It sets up an area where calculation is thrown to the winds and goods are deliberately squandered, where usefulness is forgotten and generosity reigns. Such wastefulness is, we repeat, true wealth; the wealth of the festival time. And only in this festival time can leisure unfold and come to fruition.

Separated from the sphere of divine worship, of the cult of the divine, and from the power it radiates, leisure is as impossible as the celebration of a feast. Cut off from the worship of the divine, leisure becomes laziness and work inhuman.

That is the origin or source of all sham forms of leisure with their strong family resemblance to want of leisure and to sloth (in its old metaphysical and theological sense). The vacancy left by absence of worship is filled by mere killing of time and by boredom, which is directly related to inability to enjoy leisure; for one can only be bored if the spiritual power to be leisurely has been lost. There is an entry in Baudelaire's *Journal Intime* that is fearful in the precision of its cynicism: "One must work, if not from taste then at least from despair. For, to reduce everything to a single truth: work is less boring than pleasure."

And the counterpart to that is the fact that if real leisure is deprived of the support of genuine feast days and holy days, work itself becomes inhuman: whether endured brutishly or "heroically" work is naked toil and effort without hope—it can only be compared to the labors of Sisyphus, that mythical symbol of the "worker" chained to his function, never pausing in his work, and never gathering any fruit from his labors.

In its extreme form the passion for work, naturally blind to every form of divine worship and often inimical to it, turns abruptly into its contrary, and work becomes a cult, becomes a religion. To work means to pray, Carlyle wrote, and he went on to say that fundamentally all genuine work is religion, and any religion that is not work ought to be left to Brahmins and dancing dervishes. Could anyone really pretend that that exotic nineteenth-century opinion was merely *bizarre* and not much more nearly a charter for the world of "total work"— that is on the way to becoming our world?

The celebration of divine worship, then, is the deepest of the springs by which leisure is fed and continues to be vital—though it must be remembered that leisure embraces everything which, without being *merely* useful, is an essential part of a full human existence.

In a period when divine worship is deeply felt and unites the whole social body and is, moreover, acknowledged as valid by all or nearly all, it might (perhaps) not be quite so necessary to discuss the foundation of leisure explicitly; and in so far as it was necessary to justify leisure in such periods it might (perhaps) be enough to dwell upon the purely humanistic arguments. But at a time when the nature of culture is no longer even understood, at a time when "the world of work" claims to include the whole field of human existence, and to be coterminous with it, it is necessary to go back to fundamentals in order to rediscover the ultimate justification of leisure.

An appeal to antiquity in the name of learning merely is virtually meaningless in times such as these; it is powerless against the enormous *pressure,* internal as well as external, of "the world of work." An appeal to Plato is no longer any good—unless one goes to the very roots of Plato (for we are concerned with roots, not with precedents, "influences"). Nor is it any use emphasizing that the traditions of philosophy go back to Plato's Academy, unless at the same time one accepts the religious character of the original "academy"; for Plato's Academy was a genuine religious association in which, for example, one of the members was explicitly appointed to prepare the sacrifice. Perhaps the reason' why "purely academic" has sunk to mean something sterile, pointless and unreal is *because* the *schola* has lost its roots in religion and in divine worship. And so, instead of reality we get a world of make-believe, of intellectual *trompe l'oeil,* and cultural tricks and traps and jokes, with here and there a "temple of the Muses" and a "holy of holies." Goethe certainly seems to have thought as much when he referred to the classicism of his day, in an astonishing phrase, declaring all the "*inventa* of antiquity" to be "matters *of faith*" which are now "fantastically copied out of pure fantasy."[14]

---

14. Wolfgang Goethe to Friedrich Wilhelm Riemer, March 26, 1814.

To repeat: today it is quite futile to defend the sphere of leisure in the last ditch but one. The sphere of leisure, it has already been said, is no less than the sphere of culture in so far as that word means everything that lies beyond the utilitarian world. Culture lives on religion through divine worship. And when culture itself is endangered, and leisure is called in question, there is only one thing to be done: to go back to the first and original source.

Such is, moreover, the meaning of the marvelous quotation from Plato placed at the beginning of this essay. The origin of the arts in worship, and of leisure derived from its celebration, is given in the form of a magnificent mythical image: man attains his true form and his upright attitude "in festive companionship with the gods."

But what—someone may well ask—are we *to do* about it?

Well, the considerations put forward in this essay were not designed to give advice and draw up a line of action; they were meant to make men think. Their aim has been to throw a little light on a problem which seems to me very important and very urgent, and is all too easily lost to sight among the immediate tasks in hand.

The object of this essay, then, is not to provide an immediate, practical guide to action. Nevertheless, there is one hope which ought, in conclusion, to be set down clearly— the fact is that in this sphere the decisive result is not to be achieved through action but can only be hoped for as dispensation. Our effort has been to regain some space for true leisure, to bring back a fundamentally right possession of leisure, "active leisure." The true difficulty in this often desperate effort is due to the fact that the ultimate root of leisure is not susceptible to the human will. Absolute affirmation of the universe cannot, strictly speaking, be based upon a voluntary resolve. Above all it cannot be "done" for the sake of a purpose lying outside itself. There are things that we cannot do "in order to…" or "so that…." Either we do them not at all or we do them because they are right in saying that lack of leisure makes for illness. But just as certainly it is impossible to attempt to engage in leisure for health's sake. Such a reversal of the meaningful order of things is more than just unseemly; it simply cannot be done. Leisure cannot be achieved at all when it is sought as a means to an end, even though that end be "the salvation of Western civilization." Celebration of God in worship cannot be done unless it is done for its own sake. That most sublime form of affirmation of the world as a whole is the fountainhead of leisure.

Our hope is, in the first place, that the many signs *intra et extra muros* of a reawakening of the feeling for worship and its significance should not prove deceptive and misleading. For, to recapitulate: no one need expect a genuine religious worship, a *cultus*, to arise on purely human foundations, on foundations made by man; it is of the very nature of religious worship that its origin lies in a divine ordinance, a fact which is moreover implied in the quotation from Plato already referred to. No doubt the feeling for what has been ordained and laid down may increase, or it may lose its vitality. And that is the point toward which our hopes are directed—and not, of course, to the revival of some antiquated cult; and still less toward the foundation of a new religion! From those who see no hope along these lines (and hopelessness along these lines, it must be conceded, could produce not a few grounds in its defense)—from those who see nothing worth hoping for here—we should certainly not expect to find confidence in the future. This is a matter about which it seems to me of the utmost importance to leave no doubt in their minds.

Worship is either something "given," divine worship is fore-ordained—or it does not exist at all. There can be no question of founding a religion or instituting a religious *cultus*. And for the Christian there is, of course, no doubt in the matter: *post Christum* there is only *one*, true and final form of celebrating divine worship, the sacramental sacrifice of the Christian Church. And moreover I think that anyone inquiring into the facts of the case from a historical point of view (whether he is a Christian or not) would be unable to find any other worship whatsoever in the Europeanized world.

The Christian *cultus*, unlike any other, is at once a sacrifice and a sacrament.[15] In so far as the Christian *cultus* is a *sacrifice* held in the midst of the creation which is affirmed by this sacrifice of the God-man—every day is a feast day; and in fact the liturgy knows only feast days, even working days

---

15. *Summa Theologica*, III, 79, 5.

being *feria*. In so far as the *cultus* is a *sacrament* it is celebrated in visible signs. And the full power of worship will only be felt if its sacramental character is realized in undiminished form, that is, if the sign is fully visible. In leisure, as was said, man oversteps the frontiers of the everyday workaday world, not in external effort and strain, but as though lifted above it in ecstasy. That is the sense of the visibility of the sacrament: that man is "carried away" by it, thrown into "ecstasy." Let no one imagine for a moment that that is a private and romantic interpretation. The Church has pointed to the meaning of the incarnation of the Logos in the self-same words: *ut dum visibiliter Deum cognoscimus, per hunc in invisibilium amorem rapiamur*, that we may be rapt into love of the invisible reality through the visibility of that first and ultimate sacrament: the Incarnation.

We therefore hope that this true sense of sacramental visibility may become so manifest in the celebration of the Christian *cultus* itself that in the performance of it man, "who is born to work," may truly be "transported" out of the weariness of daily labor into an unending holiday, carried away out of the straitness of the workaday world into the heart of the universe.

THE BLESSINGS OF LIBERTY

notes

notes

CLUNY MEDIA

Designed by Fiona Cecile Clarke, the CLUNY MEDIA *logo
depicts a monk at work in the scriptorium,
with a cat sitting at his feet.*

*The monk represents our mission to emulate
the invaluable contributions of the monks
of Cluny in preserving the libraries of the West,
our strivings to know and love the truth.*

*The cat at the monk's feet is Pangur Bán, from the
eponymous Irish poem of the 9th century.
The anonymous poet compares his scholarly
pursuit of truth with the cat's happy hunting of mice.
The depiction of Pangur Bán is an homage to the work
of the monks of Irish monasteries and a sign
of the joy we at Cluny take in our trade.*

"Messe ocus Pangur Bán,
cechtar nathar fria saindan:
bíth a menmasam fri seilgg,
mu memna céin im saincheirdd."